the Institute *of* Public Relations
P R I N P R A C T I C E S E R I E S

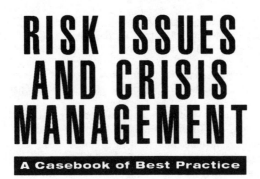
RISK ISSUES AND CRISIS MANAGEMENT

A Casebook of Best Practice

Mina
Merry Christmas
Peter
1998

The Institute of Public Relations (IPR)

The IPR is the professional body for public relations in the UK. Its role is:
- to provide a professional structure for the practice of public relations;
- to enhance the ability and status of its members as professional practitioners;
- to represent the interests of its members;
- to provide opportunities for members to meet and exchange views and ideas;
- to offer a range of services of professional and personal benefit to members.

Founded in 1948, the Institute now has over five thousand four hundred members practising in consultancies and in-house in all sectors of the UK economy. Members, whether generalist or specialist, are drawn from all areas of practice and management, up to main Board level, in industry and commerce, local and central government, in health and education services and charities, in the police and armed forces, in privatised and nationally owned utilities and services.

Membership of the Institute of Public Relations

Since January 1992 full membership (MIPR) of the Institute has been gained only by qualification combined with a period of professional experience, although for senior practitioners the qualification element may be substituted by ten years experience. The criteria established for the qualification element is to reach, both in range and depth, the standards laid down in the Public Relations Education and Training Matrix.

One consequence of this decision is that, increasingly over time, membership will comprise practitioners and managers who have a formally recognised public relations qualification.

The Institute also offers Student membership and Associate membership (AMIPR) for those on their way to full membership. Affiliate membership is for those who work in a specialised area of communication and who support the Institute's aims, but who would not be entitled to full membership. Fellowship (FIPR) is awarded to Members in recognition of outstanding work in public relations.

For further information please contact:

The Institute of Public Relations
The Old Trading House
15 Northburgh Street
London EC1V 0PR
Tel: 0171 253 5151
Fax: 0171 490 0588

the Institute *of* Public Relations

P R I N P R A C T I C E S E R I E S

RISK ISSUES AND CRISIS MANAGEMENT

A Casebook of Best Practice

Michael Regester *&* Judy Larkin

the Institute *of* Public Relations

KOGAN
PAGE

First published in 1997.

Kogan Page Limited
120 Pentonville Road
London N1 9JN

© Michael Regester and Judy Larkin, 1997

British Library Cataloguing in Publication Data
A CIP record for this book is available from the British Library.

ISBN 0 7494 2393 5

Typeset by BookEns Ltd, Royston, Herts.
Printed and bound in Great Britain by Clays Ltd, St Ives plc.

for

Paul
Leanne
Lucinda, Alice, Kimberley and Daniel

Contents

PR in Practice Series

Published in association with the Institute of Public Relations
Consultant Editor: Anne Gregory

Kogan Page has joined forces with the Institute of Public Relations to publish this unique new series which is designed specifically to meet the needs of the increasing numbers of people seeking to enter the public relations profession and the large band of existing PR professionals.

Taking a practical, action-oriented approach, the books in the series will concentrate on the day-to-day issues of public relations practice and management rather than academic theory.

They will provide ideal primers for all those on IPR, CAM and CIM courses or those taking NVQs in PR. For PR practitioners, they will provide useful refreshers and ensure that their knowledge and skills are kept up-to-date.

Anne Gregory is head of the School of Business Strategy and an assistant dean of the Faculty of Business at Leeds Metropolitan University. As former chair of the Institute of Public Relations' Education and Training Committee, Anne initiated the PR in Practice series.

Other titles in the series are:

Effective Media Relations
Michael Bland, Alison Theaker and David Wragg
Planning and Managing a Public Relations Campaign
Anne Gregory
Public Relations in Practice
Edited by Anne Gregory
Strategic Public Relations
Edited by Anne Gregory

Forthcoming titles in the series are:

A Practitioner's Guide to Implementing Public Relations
Philip Henslowe
Running a Public Relations Consultancy   Peter Hehir
Running a Public Relations Department   Mike Beard

Available from all good bookshops, or to obtain further information please contact the publishers at the address below:

Kogan Page Ltd
120 Pentonville Road
London N1 9JN
Tel: 0171 278 0433
Fax: 0171 837 6348

About the authors

Michael Regester is an international authority, author and lecturer on crisis management and is regarded as having pioneered many of the systems, procedures and training programmes which companies can put into place to handle the communication aspects of crisis situations.

His involvement in crisis management started in 1979 when, as public affairs manager for Gulf Oil Corporation, Europe, West Africa and the Middle East, he had to handle the communication aspects of one of the oil industry's worst disasters – at Bantry Bay in Ireland.

In addition to many papers on public relations and crisis communication, he is author of *Crisis Management*, published by Century Hutchinson in 1987. His second book, *Investor Relations*, co-authored with Neil Ryder, was published by Century Hutchinson in 1990. Both are the first books on their respective subjects to be published outside the USA and have sold internationally.

He is a former board member of the International Public Relations Association, a Fellow of the UK Institute of Public Relations, and a regular visiting lecturer on crisis management at British universities.

He is a founding partner of crisis and issues management consultancy, Regester Larkin.

Judy Larkin is a founding partner of Regester Larkin and has 20 years' experience in international corporate communications and marketing.

She has worked both in-house and as a consultant, primarily in research and development-driven industries such as information technology, pharmaceuticals and petrochemicals.

A former head of corporate relations for Logica plc, she has held board-level positions with a number of major UK and US consultancies.

She has collaborated with Michael Regester on many crisis management consultancy programmes and, more recently, has been responsible for devising and introducing issues management systems into a number of international corporations.

She is a member of the Institute of Public Relations, International Public Relations Association and a board member of the Issues Management Council in the United States, and is a regular writer, speaker and visiting lecturer on crisis and issues management.

Preface

As a host of political and regulatory, economic, social and technological factors shape the way organizations work and perform today, the relationship between business and society is being questioned to a much greater degree than before.

Corporate and institutional behaviour is under much closer scrutiny. In such a complex environment, organizations have to understand and respond to rapidly shifting public values, rising expectations, demands for public consultation and an increasingly intrusive media. This is particularly crucial when things go wrong. Recent examples include Brent Spar, BSE, TWA flight 800 and the outbreak of E-coli food poisoning in Scotland.

If your responsibility involves managing or advising on any facet of communication which has a bearing on corporate reputation or operational performance, this book is intended for you.

No matter how well organized and in control you may feel about your day-to-day tasks, extraneous events may suddenly place you and your colleagues in a vulnerable position.

Something as seemingly trivial as an opinion advocated in a trade publication, a minor but continuing increase in product complaints, an unsubstantiated claim about your company's performance or an apparently unconnected trend in social behaviour could have the potential to emerge as an issue, the maturing and long-term consequences of which could be devastating for your business.

Equally, the totally unexpected could happen – in the next

hour or week – in an alarmingly fast and dramatic way, creating a true crisis situation. In either case, if you are unsure of your organization's ability to anticipate the probability of such a risk actually happening, let alone have the expertise, resources and infrastructure to cope, these 11 chapters are designed to provide a practical operational framework for pre-emptive action planning.

Risk Issues and Crisis Management in Public Relations is a best practice case book, drawing on the authors' considerable experience in working alongside senior management teams from many different industry sectors and on a cross-border basis. In addition, they refer to many well-documented case study examples and assess the lessons – both positive and negative – to be learnt from each.

Research conducted on behalf of Regester Larkin among major international corporations operating in the UK highlights the lack of a systematic approach to identify, prioritize, analyse, strategize and action issues programmes among the majority of respondents.

This book attempts to define and apply the emerging discipline of issues management with particular reference to assessing and dealing with risk in a communication context. A principal focus is on techniques for anticipating, planning and proactively managing issues to minimize negative commercial impact and create competitive opportunities.

Furthermore, while there is a greater acceptance on the part of business of the need to plan and organize for potential crisis situations, the continuing failure of senior executives to seize the initiative in explaining what has happened, what is being done to sort out the mess and, crucially, how the organization feels about what has happened, is amply demonstrated in the continuing succession of damning cases that fuel the appetite of a global media and sophisticated advocacy industry.

Guidelines for anticipating, planning, preparing and training are provided together with suggestions on how they can be applied inside your organization. These are summarized from the personal advice and experience of the authors who have made a detailed study of, and been directly involved in, handling major risk issues and corporate crises.

Acknowledgements

We would like to thank our colleagues Rosie Clifford and Catherine Spaul for research and encouragement, patience and good humour.

We also thank Philip Algar and Oil and Energy Trends and Dr Stuart Smith of 3M UK plc for their help in the compilation of the case studies on pages 63–75 and 89–97.

PART 1

RISK ISSUES MANAGEMENT

1

Outside-in thinking

Who can we trust?

Business today seems to suffer from the perception that its leaders are complacent, greedy and unconcerned about the long-term welfare of their companies and the employees that have not been shown the door through downsizing. Government regulators are considered to be in the pockets of industry, examples of bureaucratic sloth. The media is widely believed to sensationalize the news as a means to establish its own agenda. Consumer activists, often considered to be agents for constructive change, are being criticized for exaggerating the dangers facing society. To understand why, it is worth examining some interesting trends affecting the changing relationship between business and society.

First, there are many dynamic forces – political and regulatory, economic, social and technological – that are shaping the way organizations work, perform and behave. They are expanding:

- the quantity, quality and speed of information globally
- the impact of new broadcast and multimedia technologies on public opinion

- the competition for reaching and influencing consumers
- the knowledge, values and behaviour of constituents
- the association between product and corporate brand reputation.

Second, the role of government and corporations in society is being challenged to a much greater degree than before. Here are some examples.

Public policy formulation is still an evolutionary process. We are quite naturally confused over government roles at local, regional, national and federal levels. This is characterized by uncertainties at a national level of the benefits of a unified Europe and the perceived responsibilities of newly democratized systems of government in central Europe.

Corporate and institutional behaviour is under much greater scrutiny. Critical media reports highlight concerns over excessive profits and senior executive pay, a lack of adequate corporate governance and corruption scandals in the financial and public services sectors. Monopolistic practices are questioned as industries consolidate and integrate for global competitiveness. 'Dirty tricks' campaigning, aggressive lobbying tactics that compromise the credibility of executives and public officials, and too much interference by business in government typify the populist braying of newspaper and broadcast editors alike.

We are less trusting of those in authority. In most developed countries, government promises on taxation and healthcare reform continue to be broken, and we are challenging industrial performance, for example, over the environmental reputation of oil and chemical companies. Even the ethical stance of companies focusing on socially responsible business practices, such as Body Shop, Ben & Jerry's and Levi Strauss, is being called to account.

Corporate loyalty is no longer a given. Redundancies, relocations, the erosion of workers' rights and job security have taken their toll. Demographic changes mean fewer young people are entering the market, the demand for skilled workers is gradually increasing while unskilled jobs are in decline. Employment is likely to become a sellers' market.

The social landscape is changing. Populations are getting older, resulting in several European countries raising the retirement age at a time when people generally want to stop work earlier. Our traditional family structures are under intense pressure. Nearly one in two marriages are ending in divorce in the UK. Coupled with declining job security, domestic property prices, pension and elderly welfare provision, a staggering change in family cash flow through an average lifecycle is illustrated in Figure 1.1.

Opinion polling in the United States and Europe indicates that some of the principal shifts occurring in society that give rise to concern relate to:

- safety and security, including economic security
- environment, including workplace
- gender/equality
- service quality/value for money
- institutional accountability
- empowerment.

Changes in these and other areas are bringing about a big increase in activism. We are now much more likely to vote with our feet on issues of major concern, by picketing, boycotting and litigating. In the past ten years, the proliferation of single-issue groups has outstripped anything in the past. Powerful and well organized, there is rarely a sandal-wearing extremist in sight. They have money and are well connected, often with sophisticated cross-border links.

This vocal and energetic movement is growing in line with corporate unpopularity, tackling issues as diverse as food and health safety, pollution, animal welfare, trading standards, smoking, ageism, racism, nuclear disarmament, sexism in the workplace, litter, noise, pornography, pesticides and disclosure of information. There are now more than 1000 single-issue campaign groups in the UK, ranging from big organizations like the multinational Greenpeace with 4,000,000 members to

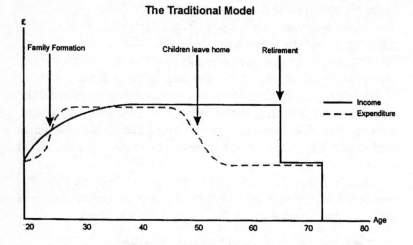

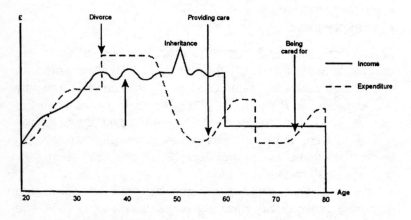

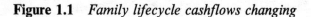

Source: Henley Centre

Figure 1.1 *Family lifecycle cashflows changing*

specialist outfits such as Surfers Against Sewage. One way or another, they have the power to inflict long-term damage on companies and, like shareholders and politicians, they need to be factored into corporate planning and decision making.

Organizations are operating in a hostile environment where their word is unlikely to be trusted. Even though Greenpeace got its facts wrong on Brent Spar, it proved to be smarter, better organized and more popular than one of Europe's largest and most respected companies. A survey by the Henley Centre found that only 15 per cent of people thought multinational corporations were trustworthy. Against this backdrop the allegations of special interest groups are likely to be believed.

In today's complex environment, organizations have to understand and respond to our rapidly shifting values, rising expectations, demands for public consultation and an increasingly intrusive news media. It is no longer enough to focus on internal objectives alone: *outside-in thinking*, illustrated in Figure 1.2, is an essential prerequisite for achieving the tacit acceptance of society to continue to operate.

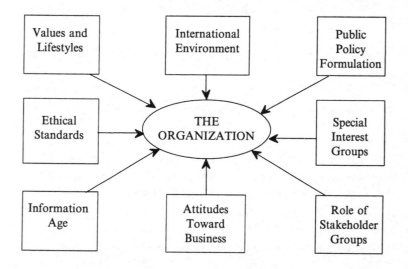

Figure 1.2 *Outside-in thinking*
Source: Ashley & Morrison

There is a growing expectation, on the part of a broad range of stakeholder groups, that organizations should perform and behave in a more open, socially caring and responsible way. These principles are even more important in times of intense pressure, for example, where there is a *real* or *perceived* risk to public health, safety or the environment.

Dealing with risk

The so-called 'Risk society thesis' identifies new patterns of political and public anxiety. This conflict is being brought about by a combination of:

- continuous societal change and uncertainty
- the remorseless pace of industrial and technological innovation
- time and cost pressures that do not allow for adequate scientific evaluation of the risks versus the benefits of new innovation
- a trend towards greater individuality and assertive public opinion.

In combination, these factors are intensifying a host of risk issues.

Traditional reliance on the judgement of experts to interpret levels of risk in using new products and processes is now parallelled by a growing ability on our part – reinforced by a modern media – to challenge political and corporate reassurance couched as scientific or technical fact. The perceived risk of contracting CJD through BSE-infected cattle is an example of the potential and real business impact of exaggerated public fear.

Risk is a measure of the adverse effect of an issue. It is about assessing and communicating the possible *hazards* associated with a particular process relative to the *safeguards* and *benefits* which it offers. This helps us, as consumers, to make choices about our health and safety, and the protection of the environment in which we live.

Risk assessment is essential when:

- a *new risk emerges* – such as the threat of contracting CJD or the safety of the Channel Tunnel following the fire in 1996
- the *degree of existing risk changes* — such as the dangers of hand guns following the Dunblane massacre in 1996 or the perceived risk of thrombosis from the newer generation contraceptive pills
- or, a *new perception of risk occurs* as in the potential impact of so-called gender-bending chemicals (phthalates) on animal and human health, and the environment.

All too often during public health and safety scares, the basis for sensible decision making has remained buried beneath an avalanche of scientific or technical data. According to US crisis management specialist, Peter McCue, each crisis follows a similar pattern:

- a special interest group sounds the alarm
- the media creates widespread awareness of the claim
- industry responds with reams of data and proclaims its products safe
- in the face of increasing shrillness, the public becomes anxious and avoids the products in question until more reliable information is available
- sales decline as regulators equivocate and issue confusing guidelines
- relying on exaggerated public fear, the activists step up the campaign
- the media faithfully covers everything they do and say
- industry reacts strenuously, occasionally resorting to exaggerations of its own in an attempt to restore calm and boost sales
- for a period of time everyone loses perspective on the issue
- eventually, a more accurate and balanced assessment emerges

- industry braces itself for another day
- those who make their living from consumerism find somewhere else to spread doom and gloom
- the media moves on to the next crisis, giving little attention to clarifications of the original inflated charge
- government returns to studying the issue so that it can write new and confusing legislation.

So, there are a number of dilemmas facing organizations endeavouring to understand and manage the dynamics of a risk issue:

- *risk means different things to different people* – we over-estimate sensational risks, like flying or contracting CJD, while we underestimate common risks such as driving a car or taking a short cut through an alley at night
- *basic attitudes are hard to change* – they are forged by a range of social and cultural factors and reinforced by our own contact with and opinions advocated by friends, colleagues, family members and others. These attitudes shape the way we interpret, understand and act upon new risks
- *the public is not looking for zero risk* – we each constantly make risk/benefit choices, consciously or unconsciously, but there is a basic unease about two things: where is the benefit and can the people responsible for managing the risk be trusted? This is particularly true in areas of food and health safety, for example in food processing, biotechnology and synthetic chemical usage
- *the source of information about risk is critical* – research in the UK indicates that consumers are totally confused about who to trust on food safety. A Mori public opinion survey after the Brent Spar incident in 1995 asking 'Who did they trust?' gave an 82 per cent score to Greenpeace, 48 per cent to Shell and 28 per cent to the UK government. A similar question in the same environmental issues poll to assess public confidence in scientists gave a 97 per cent rating to scientists working for environmental groups, compared with 77 per

cent for government scientists and 64 per cent for industry scientists (see Figure 1.3). In other words, third-party expert allies play a crucial role in risk issue management.

Public Confidence in Scientists working for...

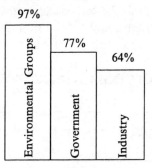

Media Confidence in Scientists working for...

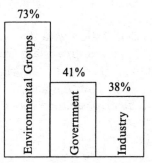

Who would you trust more to make the right decisions about the environment?

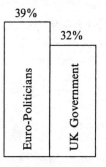

Source: Mori 1995

Figure 1.3 *Sources of information and trust*

27

- *emotion* is the most powerful influencer of all. Emotional symbols – water cannon jets aimed at Greenpeace activists attempting to occupy the Brent Spar, aerial shots of the oil spill in Alaska, the cloud hanging over Chernobyl, debris floating in the water off Long Island following the crash of TWA flight 800 and the Snowdrop campaigners at Parliament – can overwhelm and *totally negate scientific fact.*

Handling the organizational response

For organizations facing emerging risk issues, some of the principal guideposts for effective risk communication are:

- to understand the dynamics of public emotion and the working practices of special interest groups and the media who may strive to raise and legitimize a stance on an issue for public debate and, ultimately, public policy formulation
- to familiarize the organization with the cyclical development of an issue; to focus appropriate resource on early identification and monitoring of information relevant to the emerging issue and organized activity for response. This should include a clearly defined policy and associated communication strategy
- to appreciate that it is not realistic to change public opinion about the *size* of the risk (even if the true risk of an unfamiliar hazard is small), and so for the organization or industry:
  — to communicate in language that relates to and alleviates public anxiety
  — to establish and build *trust* about the commitment to *control, reduce and contain it.*

The advocacy approach

According to Howard Chase (1984), more often than not activist groups are setting the public policy agenda by combining propaganda techniques with computer-age technology.

First, they create a perceived need for their reform idea (eg, that phthalate levels in synthetic chemical manufacture are destroying our reproductive systems and the environment) in both special interest and establishment press and before groups of opinion leaders.

Second, they create the appearance of legitimacy for the idea through studies, third-party validation and, ultimately, through public opinion polling and public policy lobbying.

Finally, they use other information dissemination techniques such as widespread editorial, direct mail and grass roots mobilization to extend their viewpoint on a cross-border basis.

From a corporate perspective, our own research on issues management carried out at the end of 1995 indicates that corporations were most concerned about/involved in dealing with the types of issues shown in Figure 1.4.

At its simplest, a campaign may consist of gathering information and passing it on to the media and government.

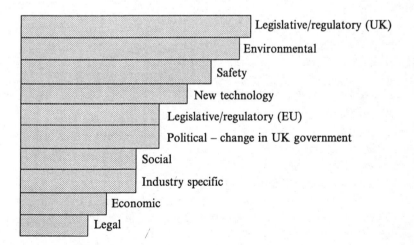

Source: Regester Larkin, 1995

Figure 1.4 *Costs and choices*

Often, by using research, a pressure group can win public support for its cause and the courts can be brought into the equation to challenge corporate performance. Members and supporters can be mobilized to write to companies complaining about actions and policies. More pressure can be exerted by a boycott. Lufthansa agreed to stop transporting animals for laboratory testing ten days after European anti-vivisection groups launched a campaign urging travellers to use another airline. The student boycott of Barclays Bank for operating in South Africa lasted 15 years, and was one factor that contributed to its eventual withdrawal in 1986.

Shareholders can also be tapped for support. Pensions and Investment Research Consultants claim there has been a rapid rise in ethical unit trusts over the last five years. Demonstrations at company annual meetings are now regular events, targeting companies such as British Gas with its 'Cedric the pig' campaign in 1995, attacking executive pay levels. Furthermore, financial institutions have experienced the damage inflicted by legal claims resulting from environmental pollution. Claims relating to toxic waste, asbestos and radioactive waste contributed about 20 per cent of the recent serious losses at the Lloyd's of London insurance market.

The new litigious culture of the late twentieth century is costing corporate America $43 billion a year in product liability insurance. Even a small high street solicitor in the UK who paid an annual premium of £1000 for professional indemnity 20 years ago, is faced with a bill of £60,000 today. The burgeoning lottery of compensation claims for personal injury – physical and emotional – is achieving Alice in Wonderland status. UK health authorities are one of many public bodies in the firing line, anticipating an annual increase of between 15 per cent and 20 per cent in compensation claims. A recent landmark judgement centred on a 20-year-old who accepted an out-of-court settlement of £30,000 over claims that he had been bullied at a school in south-west London.

In the United States, the top 12 environmental pressure groups have operating budgets totalling around $400,000,000 a year, from a donor base of around 13,000,000 contributors. That works out at over 10,000,000 more people and an extra $250,000,000 than the entire combined Democratic and Republican parties have available to them.

The volume of work created by these advocacy groups, particularly in the area of environmental protection, is forcing organizations to focus on the introduction of issues management systems and new functions to manage them. In recent years, big businesses have shifted their thinking, believing there are commercial as well as social advantages to communicating about the steps they are taking to reduce their impact on precious resources without redressing the imbalance in some way. Many companies now publish environmental policy statements and employ specialists to devise strategies for cleaning up manufacturing processes and developing environmental initiatives in the community. Similarly, some organizations are implementing marketing and sponsorship programmes designed to promote brand awareness but in an ethically sustainable manner. 'Advocacy advertising' and 'cause-related marketing' campaigns are run by companies such as Levi Strauss, Benetton, J&B, Body Shop and many retail banks.

In his book, *The Critical Issues Audit* (1994), Eli Sopow refers to news content analysis research which shows a consistent pattern by advocacy groups or individuals who are attempting to gain public support for their action. The steps are listed below and shown in Figure 1.5.

Step 1: A key point of conflict is established, generally presented in simple terms. Action words are used by advocates to create a sense of urgency. Those words include *unique, new, first, only, last.*

Step 2: Once the issue has been identified as important/urgent it requires legitimacy. This is provided through apparent scientific and technical confirmation, with action words like *research, evidence, studies, tests.*

Step 3: The issue now has a sharp focus, and is backed up with scientific research. This step incorporates the necessary ingredient of broad-based public support. Action words are *people say, public demand, strong support.*

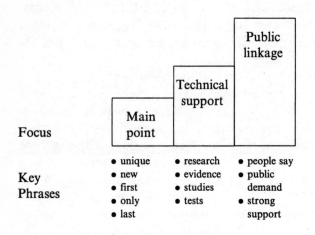

Focus

Key
Phrases

	Main point	Technical support	Public linkage
	• unique	• research	• people say
	• new	• evidence	• public
	• first	• studies	demand
	• only	• tests	• strong
	• last		support

Source: Sopow, E (1994) *The Critical Issues Audit*

Figure 1.5   *Advocacy approach*

In formulating a potential strategy relating to an emerging issue, it is possible to anticipate some of the types of tactics that advocacy groups are likely to adopt. These tactics help to mobilize public opinion in such a way that pressure for public policy change – ie greater industry regulation – can be brought to bear.

Using our phthalates example, these tactics will include:

- advocating, through the media and independent scientific experts, the need for a (long-term) comprehensive and independently commissioned research programme (to be funded by government and industry) to established 'benchmark criteria'; the aim is to pressurize government to take action to eliminate synthetic chemicals that disrupt hormones and a key objective here is to shift the burden of proof to chemical manufacturers
- proposing the development of a model similar to the 1987 Montreal Protocol, an international treaty that mandates the phase-out of CFCs and other ozone-depleting chemicals on an international basis (see Chapter 4).

In addition, advocacy groups could encourage activists at grass roots level via calls to:

- prevent exposure to hormone-disrupting chemicals through their total elimination

- regulate every new compound so that before it is allowed to enter commercialization it is subjected to tests by manufacturers to ascertain what risks the chemicals pose

- protect against the vulnerability of children and the unborn, taking into account that the effects of exposure on developmental processes are usually irreversible

- change specific regulations and laws to take into account the additive and interactive effects of chemicals, not simply the effects of each individual chemical

- assess contaminant levels from any single source within the context of total cumulative exposure rather than on an individual basis

- manufacturers to provide comprehensive labels for their products so consumers have the information they need to protect themselves and their families from hormonally-active compounds

- force manufacturers/distributors to accept responsibility for monitoring their products for contamination

- companies to detail the quantity of hormone-disrupting compounds incorporated into their products

- collate comprehensive records of birth defects and symptoms of impaired function to determine whether significant changes are occurring

- force governments to collaborate cross-border to act in the face of a genuine threat to human welfare.

So, the industry or organizational 'issue action plan' needs to factor in the methods of working and approaches of special interest groups in order to effectively respond to this type of agenda setting. In addition, companies now need to be taking steps to actively consult with the communities of which they are a part.

Public consultation – building dialogue into the communications process

In today's disaffected political environment, leaders in government and business are being called upon to embrace genuine public input. Public consultation is an increasingly important facet of *outside-in thinking*. It is about building dialogue into the communications process to minimize conflict and to achieve as much consensus as possible in balancing the scales of protectionism and developmentalism.

Simply assuming that being aware of upcoming issues, distributing some literature, placing some ads and holding a few 'town hall' meetings would create the result the company wanted in the first place, is fast becoming outdated. Public concern over what constitutes 'sustainable development' will continue to increase. As we learn more about the real pressures on the environment, it is argued that many of us will feel a desire to push for a slow-down in the remorseless progress of industrialization. The result is that a company's well researched and very reasonable proposal relating to seeking planning permission for a new development on the edge of a green belt area may not seem so reasonable to people who already feel threatened by environmental degradation.

We were involved in such a case in 1996, when a company waiting for confirmation of planning permission to operate a low-level radioactive waste facility was confronted – much to its surprise – by a well-organized, articulate and highly vocal local community campaign. In spite of stressing that the type of waste that would be stored at the facility posed virtually no risk to human health, local teachers, parents, children and government officials, already living in a catchment area of research establishments working with nuclear materials, felt that enough was enough. One more facility, however safe it might be, was one too many in the risk/benefit equation. Anxiety over the perceived additional risk to their health and that of the environment, and a failure on the part of the organization involved to develop a more proactive public consultation process during the application for planning permission, created mistrust and a militant response. Parents and children marched on the premises of the company, under the watchful eye of local television, radio and newspaper reporters. Although we don't expect zero risk, we do want to get as close to it as possible.

Summary

The difficulty for companies setting off down a more assertive public consultation route is that they should be prepared not to get their own way on every occasion. Unsuccessful consultation can actually polarize or further divide public opinion. Nevertheless, taking an active role in communicating about issues through adopting a more 'inclusive' approach in the influencing and consultation process will, we believe, prove to be an essential requirement if the current fault-line between financial and sustainable success is to be removed.

Outside-in thinking depends on an organization's ability to move away from one-way information flow towards active *dialogue* with a wide range of stakeholder groups. Institutions and companies, upon which we depend to provide and protect, must run much faster both to resolve potential conflict *and* achieve consensus about their role and relationship in society. Those who fail to address the need for this type of change, as we shall illustrate in the following chapters, may simply forfeit their licence to operate.

2

Issues management defined

As we described in the previous chapter, organizations are running just to stay in place in their chosen markets as rapidly shifting public values, rising expectations, demands for public consultation and an increasingly intrusive news media present greater challenges.

A recent US public opinion survey of 1000 consumers showed that half had actively boycotted a company at some time, with a further 26 per cent saying they had joined a boycott within the past year. Their outrage was caused by bad customer service, poor quality products and environmentally unsound actions. They objected to corporations whose values were out of synch with their own. The mismatch between political and public priorities, as we shall see in the following chapters, is even more pronounced. The actions of politicians and political institutions today are inconsistent with changing public attitudes leading to greater frustration, anxiety and lack of trust in the integrity and effectiveness of elected officials (Sopow, 1994).

How issues are handled can mean the difference between a crisis out of control and a proactive solution – between profit and loss. From our own experience, many issues can be anticipated and successfully managed. On the negative side, however, many organizations still fail to see there is a problem.

What is issues management?

Issues management has been around for almost 20 years, but while it has been adopted by some major corporations as a powerful strategic planning tool, it has not attracted the widespread attention we believe it deserves.

In the mid 1970s, an atmosphere of increased hostility towards corporations led business communicators to rethink the role of corporate communication. The groundswell of public suspicion about private sector management was reflected through two trends. While some 40 years ago public opinion surveys reflected a clear majority in favour of the practices of business management (an 85 per cent score was typical), 35 years on that figure had slumped to around 10–15 per cent. During the same period companies, increasingly subject to criticism, hired public relations firms in droves to defend them in the face of growing public opposition. Budgets grew tenfold, running into billions of dollars annually, but this did nothing to stop the decline of public support for corporate enterprise.

Issues management was an attempt to define the strategies that companies needed to use to counter the efforts of activist groups which were putting pressure on legislators for stricter controls of business activity. 'Despite the billions of dollars companies and their associations have spent on *external relations* business in general has been ineffective in defining and then validating its position on public policy issues' (Jones and Chase, 1979). So, a new area of corporate communication emerged – issues management was first implemented as a way in which companies could deal with their critics.

In 1978, the US Public Affairs Council defined it as 'a program which a company uses to increase its knowledge of the public policy process and enhance the sophistication and effectiveness of its involvement in that process'. Heath and Cousino offer their own explanation of issues management as 'a product of activism and the increasing inter- and intra-industry pressures by corporations to define and implement corporate social responsibility (CSR) – as well as the debate in public about what the standard of CSR should be' (1990).

Many saw the early role of issues management in the United States as an effective means to avoid large sums of clean-up money and a way to forestall incoming government legislation on employment and other social issues.

Tradition has it that in 1977 W Howard Chase coined the term 'issue management'. Chase drew upon his experience at American Can Company and the lead of another specialist who introduced the term 'advocacy advertising' to recommend a new kind of corporate communication response to the critics of business activities. Companies were advised to move from an information base to an advocacy position because 'companies should not be the silent children of society' (Chase, 1984). Since then, the relationship between business and society has become an important strategic factor in reputational and financial performance terms.

Chase and his colleague Barry Jones defined issues management as a tool which companies could use to identify, analyse and manage emerging issues (in a populist society experiencing discontinuous change) and respond to them *before* they became public knowledge. They felt that most companies reacted after the fact and were forced to accept what new regulations and guidelines were given to them.

> When challenged by today's activism, business tends to react to overt symptoms, rather than by identifying and analyzing fundamental causes of the trend which has led to a critical issue. It is not surprising, then, that when a critical issue reaches the public policy decision-making point, business finds itself the defendant in the court of public opinion.
>
> (Jones and Chase, 1979)

Public policy also needs defining and one expert says:

> Public policy is a specific course of action taken collectively by society or by a legitimate representative of society, addressing a specific problem of public concern, that reflects the interests of society or particular segments of society.
>
> (Buchholz, 1988)

Some experts describe the formation of public policy in terms of the interplay of government, the media and the public. As an issue gains momentum, a climate of opinion is created that puts pressure on government to do something about it. If, however, interest flags in any one of the three components then the issue will lose momentum (Ito, 1993).

Any section of society can and will exert some sort of pressure on government and its influence over corporations. Jones and Chase describe the formation of public policy as the result of interaction between public and private points of view. They state that a corporation has every moral and legal right to help formulate public policy instead of waiting for governments to pass legislation. As a result, more organizations, particulary in the United States, see issues management as an integral part of strategic planning and a basic ingredient for corporate survival.

Hainsworth, in a 1990 article describes the importance of issues management:

> Where legislation and regulation are concerned, issues are always resolved to someone's advantage and to someone's disadvantage. If it is the object of corporate management to maximize the organization's profits and minimize its losses in a socially responsible manner, then issues management should be seen as a critical element in overall corporate planning and management.

What about the sceptics?

Critics of the term 'issues management' feel that it implies manipulation – 'of conditions or events which are the natural and freely occurring output of a pluralistic society' (Brown, 1979). Others argue that no organizational management can will its environment to stand still, nor can it decide the direction in which the environment will change.

Scepticism about adopting issues management as a clearly defined function exists in the following areas according to tucker and Brown:

financial risk – the link between issues management and the bottom line is a tenuous one, normally only realizing benefit over the long term, if at all
boundaries — issues-based communication is just one tool used in conjunction with, for example, research, corporate planning, change management and other media and communication activities. It is both difficult to define and evaluate in isolation
diversity — the people actively conducting and taking part in the issues management function are not only from public relations backgrounds; they may include lawyers, corporate planners and analysts, reearchers, etc. It may be inappropriate to assume that the public relations practitioner is the single driving force behind issues management.

Furthermore, some specialists question the degree to which a disciplined acceptance of and approach to issues management is actually applied inside the organization.

Recent research conducted across a sample of major public corporations in the UK on behalf of our own consultancy (Regester Larkin) indicated that while there was acknowledgement by corporate communication and public affairs functions of the importance of managing issues, only 10 per cent of the sample considered that their senior management proactively dealt with issues as part of the strategic planning process. Less than 5 per cent considered their organization applied an integrated approach – linking planning, communication, regulatory and other appropriate functions – to assess, prioritize and plan for the potential impact of near- and long-term issues on corporate objectives. Ninety-five per cent of the sample felt that issues were handled in a reactive and ad hoc manner, often to the detriment of reputational and financial performance goals.

However, academic research and practical case study

examples do demonstrate that effective use of issues management techniques can:

- increase market share
- enhance corporate reputation
- save money, and
- build important relationships.

Failure to do so can lead to market share erosion, impact reputation, incur significant expense, put management in a negative spotlight and reduce corporate independence through increased regulation.

Newspaper articles quoting 'exploding toilets and a public relations disaster of epic proportions' surrounding the refit of the QE2 ocean liner at the end of 1994, demonstrated how an issue can develop to a point where financial performance and corporate reputation are negatively affected.

Having worked across both areas for many years, our experience tells us that issues management is not crisis management and the two terms should not be used interchangeably. Part of the difficulty in defining and understanding the principles of issues management is that it is less action-oriented and more anticipatory in nature than crisis management. Issues management is proactive in that it tries to identify the potential for change and influence decisions relating to that change before it has a negative effect on a corporation. Crisis management tends to be a more reactive discipline dealing with a situation *after* it becomes public knowledge and affects the company. It is needed after there is public outrage.

Dealing with crisis situations is much more immediate and we've learned to have an overnight bag at the ready wherever we are. There is normally a clear focus, and a finite set of actions and audiences and information that needs to be communicated within a short timescale. With issues management, organizations should be aiming to eliminate any possibility of outrage, often by trying to anticipate trends, changes and events that may have a bearing on the ability of the corporation to continue to operate or, indeed, achieve competitive benefit.

Issues management involves looking into the future to identify potential trends and events that *may* influence the way an organization is able to operate but which currently *may* have little real focus, probably no sense of urgency and an unclear reference in time.

According to US issues management specialists, Tucker and Broom (1993):

> Issues management is the management process whose goal is to help preserve markets, reduce risk, create opportunities and manage image (corporate reputation) as an organisational asset for the benefit of both an organisation and its primary shareholders.

What is an issue?

It will come as no surprise to discover that there are many definitions of an issue offered by business communicators and academics on both sides of the Atlantic.

An issue arises, according to US specialists Hainsworth and Meng, (1988)

> as a consequence of some action taken, or proposed to be taken, by one or more parties which may result in private negotiation and adjustment, civil or criminal litigation, or it can become a matter of public policy through legislative or regulatory action.

Chase and Jones describe an issue as 'an unsettled matter which is ready for decision'. Others suggest that in its basic form, an issue can be defined as a point of conflict between an organization and one or more of its audiences. A simple definition that we like to use is that an issue represents 'a gap between corporate practice and stakeholder expectations'. In other words, an emerging issue is a condition or event, either internal or external to the organization, that if it continues will have a significant effect on the functioning or performance of the organization or on its future interests.

Example triggers for issues management include the potential for new legislation, an opinion or claim advocated through the media or other channels, a competitive development, published research, a change in the performance or behaviour of the organization itself or individuals or groups to whom it is linked.

Managing issues frequently involves dealing with change. An overall aim is to bring some control to the impact caused by discontinuity in the environment (Heath & Nelson, 1986). The ultimate goal, according to Hainsworth and Meng, is to shape public policy to the benefit of the organization through:

- early identification of the potential impact of the change, and
- organized activity, based on sound management principles and techniques, and allowing time for analysis and creative thinking to influence the evolution and, ultimately, the outcome of that change.

It is important to remember, however, that managing issues should not be considered a defensive activity. Although most of the time we are asked to advise companies on how to minimize the commercial risks associated with change, positive opportunities for repositioning a product or process, or communicating new benefits do exist *if they are looked for*. The creation of new issues or the gathering and management of information and opinion relating to an issue can be harnessed by an organization for significant competitive or social advantage.

Who should practise issues management?

A major question relating to issues management is who is best placed to practise it? Chase feels that issues management derives strength from public relations, and from its various disciplines – public affairs, communications and government relations. He goes on to say that issues management is the highway along which public relations practitioners can move into full participation in management decision-making (Chase, 1984).

> Public relations practitioners understand that they are expected to play increasingly complex and involved roles in promoting the bottom line, building harmonious relations with stockholders, and protecting corporate interests in ways that must be sensitive to the needs of a variety of external interests.
>
> (Heath and Cousino, 1990)

We believe public relations practitioners are well placed to help manage issues effectively but often lack the necessary access to strategic planning functions or an appropriate networking environment which encourages informal as well as formal contact and reporting.

What are the functions required of issues management?

The US Public Affairs Council (1978) states that the functions required for issues management are identifying issues and trends, evaluating their impact and setting priorities, establishing a company position, designing company action and response to help achieve the position and implementing the plans.

These functions must occur constantly and be integrated and focused on the central task of helping the organization – through its management. The key tasks of this activity are *planning, monitoring, analysing* and *communicating*.

Heath and Cousino (1990) identify four broad functional requirements for a company to maximize its position and positively sustain its public policy environment, with a principal focus on nurturing relationships with stakeholders. These are described below.

Smart planning and operations

If issues managers are doing a good job of capturing the critical changes in the public policy environment then that information should be integrated into the strategic business plan and corporate management strategies. The rationale is that this kind of information can offer business opportunities, justify the curtailment or change of business activities, and guide the standards by which the company operates. 'Issues management can positively affect corporate performance by enhancing the firm's responsiveness to environmental change' (Wartick and Rude, 1986).

Tough defence and smart offence

Issues management offers the rationale, tools and incentives for becoming involved in the discussion of public policy issues as early as possible. If companies get involved before issues have solidified, they can increase the likelihood of their communication campaigns succeeding. In other words, what needs to be said to whom and with what intended effect to exert influence in the public policy arena?

Getting the house in order

According to the authors this is about examining requirements to achieve appropriate commitments to matters of corporate social responsibility. Research in the United States found that market forces alone do not shape the fate of corporations – public policy change plays its role. In addition, public affairs must be sensitive to public policy forces and assist in corporate planning and in the formation of business ethics. The essence of being a responsive organization in the modern world is to move from coping with external demands to anticipating how demands can best be met within the technical and economic context of the organization (Post and Kelley, 1988).

Scouting the terrain

What companies believe to be the nature of the marketplace is likely to influence their strategic business plans. The same can be said of businesses that use issues monitoring to assess the public policy environment. Greater sophistication has been used in an effort to refine strategic management information systems. In addition to straightforward polls and surveys, futurists, for example, have used social scientific techniques to offer valuable insights into the ways issues can be identified, monitored and analysed. The key to making this activity effective is understanding a corporation's culture, its organizational and political structures and the nature of public policy issues analysis. Companies can then determine what issues to monitor and analyse as they refine their public policy and strategic plans. This process requires more than periodic public opinion surveys.

Summary

The importance of anticipation – forward-thinking skills inside the organization – and outside-in thinking skills in relation to the role of new and diverse stakeholders, should not be underestimated. The push towards globalization and the requirement for organizations and institutions to understand and respond to the sophisticated demands of consumers and constituents, emphasize the critical connection between business and society in the decades ahead.

While practical experience demonstrates that barriers exist to understanding, resourcing and managing the impact of change in the future, we are convinced that the implications of failing to examine the farthest reaches of the lighthouse loom – how issues emerge, mature and are resolved at a political, regulatory, economic, social or technological level – can deprive an organization or an industry of its ability to continue to sustain a viable existence. Equally, evidence exists to suggest that organizations can gain influence and commercial advantage through positively shaping the progress of trends, conditions and events which spawn issues. The rationale for anticipation, planning and progression to minimize risk and capitalize on opportunities in the issues arena are explored in the next chapters.

3

Planning an issues management programme – an issues management model

Issues generally evolve in a predictable manner, originating from trends or events and developing through a sequence of identifiable stages that are not dissimilar to the cyclical development of a product. Because the evolution of an issue often results in changes in public policy, the earlier a relevant issue can be identified and managed in terms of a systematic organisational response, the more likely it is that the organisation can resolve conflict and minimise cost implications to its advantage. For this reason, understanding the cyclical development of an issue is critical to effective issues management (Hainsworth, 1990).

Meng (1987) identifies six possible groups or publics that make issues: associates, employee associations, the general public, government, media and special or general interest groups. Their influence on organizations may vary from controlling the operations of a company to forming internal and external coalitions to increase the potential influence of an issue. So, when issues are ready for decision, organizational response can be critical. Meng characterises issues into several types: demographic, economic, environmental, governmental, international, public attitudes, resources, technological, and values and lifestyles.

An issue originates as an idea that has potential impact on some organization or public and may result in action that brings about increased awareness and/or reaction on the part of other organisations or publics (Hainsworth, 1990). In a model developed by Hainsworth, 1990 and Meng, 1992, this process can be described as a cycle made up of four stages: origin, mediation and amplification, organization, and resolution. In Figure 3.1, the vertical axis of the diagram represents the level of pressure

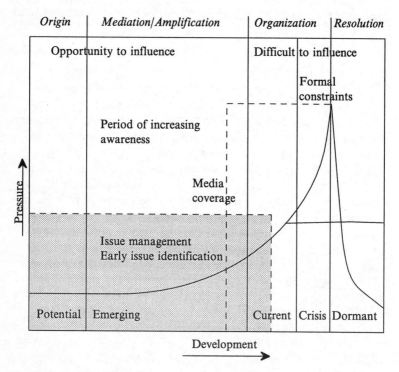

Source: Hainsworth and Meng

Figure 3.1 *Issue lifecycle*

exerted on an organization by a developing issue; the horizontal axis represents the various stages of development. At each stage of evolution pressure mounts on the organization to respond because of the increasing importance of the issue. An issue can fail at any point in the process for any number of reasons, but issues that continue to mature appear to consistently evolve from one stage to the next.

Issue lifecycle

Stage 1 – origin: potential issue

An issue arises when an organization or group attaches significance to a perceived problem (or opportunity) that is a consequence of a developing political/regulatory, economic or social trend (Crable & Vibbert, 1985). From a management perspective, trends must be identified from which issues at some point may emerge. Trends probably first become identified and articulated by academics or specialists participating in working groups, policy and planning units, who may become concerned with some problem, situation or event that has potential impact and demands response from an institution, organization, industry or other group. If a response is forthcoming, it frequently results in counter-responses from those benefiting from the status quo and those desiring change.

An issue begins to gain definition when an organization or group plans to do something that has a consequence for another organization or group (Grunig & Hunt, 1984). Awareness and concern on the part of a group brings about a resolve to 'do something'. Lines become drawn and conflict emerges (Crable & Vibbert, 1985).

So, what we see in the early *potential* stage is a defined condition or event which has the potential to develop into something of importance. The types of issues which exist in this phase, however, have not yet captured significant expert or public attention, although some specialists will begin to be aware of them.

From our own experience in the healthcare sector, an example could be a trend in the increased incidence of a disease or knowledge of forthcoming research that highlights adverse side effects of a drug. At this stage, however, the issue often lacks sufficient form or substance to justify deliberate external intervention, for example by competitors who seek to shape or redirect it. Issues that make it past Stage 1 are alive, have a momentum of their own, and are capable of being modified as they move towards resolution.

In Stage 1, groups or individuals generally begin to establish a certain level of credibility in areas of concern and seek out support from other influencers and opinion leaders who are involved to some degree in that particular area of interest. At this point it is common for those involved to feel a bit uneasy as they begin to recognize that, in some situations, a point of conflict could exist.

> The constant scanning of this process and early identification of potential issues is important and should be an integral part of the corporate planning process itself.
>
> (Nagy Hanna, 1985)

Stage 2 – mediation and amplification: emerging issue

As groups emerge and lines become drawn, a process of mediation and amplification occurs among other individuals and groups who may have a similar viewpoint and may be expected to react in a similar way. Initially, this takes place within the relevant specialist media of interest groups, industries, professions and others with comparable opinions, values or concerns. As momentum builds within the mass media, the issue becomes amplified into a public issue that may become part of the public policy process.

The *emerging* issue stage indicates a gradual increase in the level of pressure on the organization to accept the issue. In most cases, this increase is the result of activities by one or more groups as they try to push or legitimize the issue (Meng, 1987). Using our healthcare example, this may involve competitors of a pharmaceutical company using published data to gather support from opinion leaders and influencers such as the media to gain medical community and, ultimately, public/patient acceptance of *their* interpretation of the issue.

At this stage in the issue's development it is still relatively easy for the organization to intervene and play a proactive role in preventing or exploiting the evolution of the issue. However, it is often difficult to determine the urgency of the issue, and we have often found the issue slipping away at this point as management attention evaporates in favour of more immediate and pressing matters. Although it is hard to know whether the issue will remain moderate or increase in intensity, stay confined to a particular area or become pervasive, it can be folly simply to pursue the status quo. We have seen this in recent public health scares and in increasingly persistent and professionally organized grass roots campaigning on animal welfare and environmental issues.

A dominant factor in the development of the issue in this phase is media coverage. Frequent editorial, initially specialist/trade and then broader general/business, begins before the issue reaches the shaded area in Figure 3.1. Before the issue reaches the next stage, those involved usually try to attract media attention as a means of progressing the issue. Sporadic in the beginning, this coverage will eventually become regular and is a critical factor to be considered in the advancement of the issue (Meng, 1987). Time and time again we have been involved in situations where regular competitor assessment, early media scanning and the decision to communicate with the media have happened too late.

According to Hainsworth the process of mediation is critical and has the effect of accelerating the full development of the issue. It is therefore essential that companies which are targeted conduct regular and effective monitoring of the commercial, regulatory and social environment in order to identify Stage 2 issues and begin to formulate action plans to deal with them.

Stage 3 – organization: current and crisis issue

Mediation brings varying degrees of organization. Positions solidify. Groups begin to seek a resolution to the conflict that is either acceptable to their best interests or at least minimizes potential damage.

In the context of the public policy process, publics or groups should be viewed as dynamic. They are often groups of individuals with varying degrees of commitment who face a similar problem, recognize that the problem exists and unite in some way to do something about the problem (Hainsworth, 1990). These groups are not static and their level of organization, funding and media literacy can vary enormously. At one end of the spectrum, they may be informal networks of people sharing only one passing interest in the resolution of the conflict, or they may be highly organized, well-connected and funded with an intense and focused commitment.

As these groups work out their viewpoints and objectives and seek to communicate their respective positions, conflict achieves a level of public visibility that is likely to push the issue into the public policy process (Hainsworth, 1990). In turn, increased public attention motivates influential leaders to become a part of the emerging conflict and pressure mounts on institutional bodies to seek a resolution to the conflict.

An example of this process was the establishment of the Snowdrop Campaign in the UK in 1996 which called for a ban on hand guns in the aftermath of the Dunblane massacre. The impact of an individual can be equally effective. In early 1997, a village resident campaigned successfully against his local parish council in Yorkshire, England to protect 56 yards of hawthorn hedge from being removed to develop a bowling green, with knock-on implications for the protection of 40,000 miles of hedgerow in the UK.

In the *current* phase, the issue has matured and is displaying its full potential upon those involved. It becomes very difficult to affect the issue as it has now become enduring, pervasive and increasing in its intensity. The different parties involved recognize its full importance and, in response, place pressure on regulatory institutions to become involved.

As the issue lifecycle diagram illustrates, in no time at all the issue ramps up from *current* to *crisis* status to reach a formal institution such as a regulatory authority which has the power to intervene and impose constraints on the organization or industry as a way to resolve the situation. This was clearly demonstrated by Exxon Corporation's perceived failure to move swiftly enough to clean up the Exxon Valdez oil spill in Alaska in 1989, which led to stiff public policy requirements for ocean-going oil tankers to be built with two hulls.

Similarly, looking at our pharmaceutical industry example, there could be demands for additional safety data through costly new patient trials, blacklisting of specific drugs restricting patient indications, major changes in prescribing information, company-funded patient education programmes and, ultimately, product withdrawal. Options available to the organization to affect or influence the issue are now limited – it is in crisis response mode.

In 1982, Eli Lilly became the target of international media attention and protracted, costly litigation associated with the withdrawal of the anti-arthritic drug, Opren. With claims that the drug caused unpleasant side-effects, including persistent photosensitivity, the company was forced into significant out-of-court settlements valued at millions of pounds.

Hundreds more alleged victims of the banned drug sought compensation some ten years later, but the courts ruled that the majority of claimants had initiated their actions too late. The issue continued to be the focus of adverse media commentary, citing elderly arthritic sufferers attempting to seek compensation from an unsympathetic pharmaceutical giant.

Arguably, if Eli Lilly had moved more quickly to present an efficacy and safety database that could refute the severity of the claims being made against Opren and mobilized supportive opinion leaders to present a balanced case via the media, the company could have avoided such long-term negative consequences.

Stage 4 – resolution: dormant issue

Once issues receive the attention of public officials and enter the policy process, either through changes to legislation or regulation, efforts to resolve the conflict become protracted and costly, as illustrated by the tobacco industry. The object of the public policy process is the imposition of unconditional constraints on all parties to the conflict – either to their advantage or to their disadvantage (Hainsworth, 1990).

So, once an issue has run the full course of its lifecycle, it will reach a height of pressure that forces an organization to accept it unconditionally. The pervasiveness of anti-smoking legislation in the United States can be viewed as an example of this stage.

The following case study demonstrates this cyclical development of an issue and the implications of a slow organizational response.

The case of the faulty chip

Before long the majority of households in Britain will have a personal computer, a domestic appliance to be trusted much like a washing machine or fridge. Consider, then, the sense of betrayal if the computer gets it wrong. Intel, the company that makes nine out of ten of the microprocessors that go into PCs went through that nightmare in 1994. Pentium, the company's new high performance microprocessor chip, occasionally failed to come up with the right answer in complex division calculations. The errors were rare but costly, resulting in a write-off of £306,000,000 and a dented reputation.

The academic and the Internet

At Lynchberg College, Virginia, in the United States mathematics professor Thomas Nicely discovered the Pentium bug. His moment of fame came as he completed a complicated long division early one morning in June 1994. He always liked to double check his sums by hand but for some reason this time it simply wasn't working out.

According to Professor Nicely: 'Intel's tech support desk said they had never heard of it. They said they would speak to an engineering group and return my call later; in fact we did exchange calls for a period of six days or so but they never came up with any explanation or acknowledged that the error actually occurred.'

So, Professor Nicely did what any self-respecting American mathematician would do and raised the alarm to users of the Internet. He found he was not alone.

He continued: 'Within two or three days I started getting reports back that nearly all of their machines made the same error and that they came to the same conclusion as I did. It was an error in the floating point unit of the Pentium chip.'

The timing could not have been worse for Intel. The company had decided to target the lucrative home computer market with a major international advertising campaign promoting the versatility of an 'Intel inside' PC for educational, recreational and business use. The Pentium was Intel's newest and fastest chip and the advertising campaign was aimed straight at the business customers who now bought computers for their homes. Intel was becoming a consumer company – its transformation was one of the big technology success stories of the 1990s.

The corporate response

Intel's first reaction to the saga, however, looked more like a backward step. The company offered customers replacement chips but only if they could prove they did sums affected by the bug. In December 1994, however, IBM forced Intel's hand by saying the bugs were worse than reported and suspending shipments of all IT products containing Pentium microprocessors.

According to the editor of a leading UK computer magazine: 'IBM are a blue chip company and people pay a premium, corporations especially, for their machines. IBM were simply protecting their reputation as a quality supplier and at the time they were quite right in saying not enough was known about the bug.'

A senior IT systems specialist at Thorn EMI added: 'Once we determined that the faulty chip might occasionally do its sums wrong, we wouldn't know when it would happen again because it was dependent on particular combinations and particular sums. But the very fact that it might happen was enough to shake our confidence in the machines and I really couldn't afford to run with machines that potentially might get their sums wrong.'

The impact of public pressure

For Intel it was time for retreat and the company finally agreed that anyone with a Pentium-based machine could have a new chip. The cost amounted to £306,000,000.

In Silicone Valley, California, there was no doubt in people's mind that Intel was losing the public relations battle. The company was being forced by media and industry pressure into an expensive

U-turn that left a golden reputation tarnished. It was a real object lesson in how an issue ignored can turn quickly into a crisis.

Professor Kevin Keller of Stanford University summed it up: 'The two keys are to be swift and to be sincere in how you handle it and I think in both cases they (Intel) were a little bit lacking.

When he was asked by reporters how much damage the incident had caused to the company, Andy Grove, Chief Executive Officer of Intel, acknowledged the company had failed to understand the psychology of the market. Although Intel was renowned for quality and reliability, 'some place we crossed over the line to where there are millions of consumers out there who think they are better able to judge quality than we are and we were insensitive to that'. The whole issue is summarized in Figure 3.2.

Interestingly, in early 1996 when Intel was charged with misleading customers by advertising an inaccurate, higher transaction processing speed for its latest Pentium micropro-cessor, the company moved extremely quickly to make a public apology and change its promotional materials.

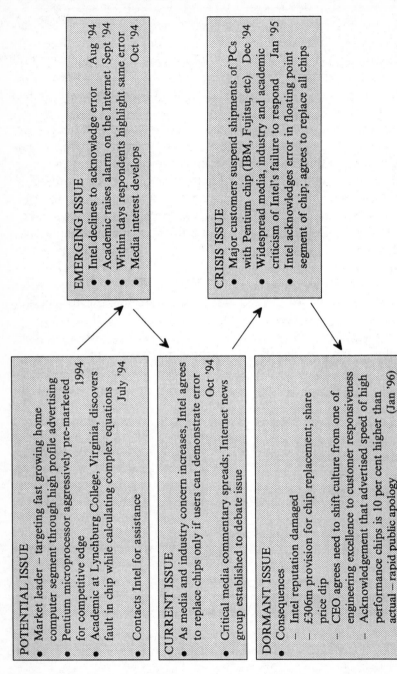

Figure 3.2 *Intel–Pentium chip*

POTENTIAL ISSUE
● Market leader – targeting fast growing home computer segment through high profile advertising
● Pentium microprocessor aggressively pre-marketed for competitive edge   1994
● Academic at Lynchburg College, Virginia, discovers fault in chip while calculating complex equations   July '94
● Contacts Intel for assistance

CURRENT ISSUE
● As media and industry concern increases, Intel agrees to replace chips only if users can demonstrate error   Oct '94
● Critical media commentary spreads; Internet news group established to debate issue

DORMANT ISSUE
● Consequences
    – Intel reputation damaged
    – £306m provision for chip replacement; share price dip
    – CEO agrees need to shift culture from one of engineering excellence to customer responsiveness
    – Acknowledgement that advertised speed of high performance chips is 10 per cent higher than actual – rapid public apology   (Jan '96)

EMERGING ISSUE
● Intel declines to acknowledge error   Aug '94
● Academic raises alarm on the Internet Sept '94
● Within days respondents highlight same error
● Media interest develops   Oct '94

CRISIS ISSUE
● Major customers suspend shipments of PCs with Pentium chip (IBM, Fujitsu, etc)   Dec '94
● Widespread media, industry and academic criticism of Intel's failure to respond   Jan '95
● Intel acknowledges error in floating point segment of chip; agrees to replace all chips

The importance of early action

The principal goal of issue identification is to place initial priorities on emerging issues. They can be classified by type (social, economic, political, technological), response source (industry, corporation, subsidiary, department), geography, span of control and salience (immediacy, prominence). Factors such as degree of impact and also the probability that the issue will mature within a reasonably predictable period of time also need to be considered.

Using the Chase/Jones Issues Management Process Model, once emerging issues have been identified and prioritized, the *issue analysis* stage begins. The aim here is to determine the origin of the issue which is often difficult as few emerge neatly from one source. The authors recommend that existing qualitative and quantitative research should be examined *before* committing to new research and that experience – past and present, internal and external to the organization – should be tapped into. Analysing the present situation will determine the current *intensity* of the issue. Applied research about the relationship of the issue to the corporation should be targeted towards opinion leaders and media gatekeepers. This initial research and analysis stage will help to identify what influential individuals and groups are saying about the issues and provide management with a clear idea of their *origin* and *evolution*.

Needless to say, in practice we have found great reluctance to spend money on this type of research as part of the benchmarking and planning process. Where possible, we try to develop arguments in terms of impact on financial performance and risk to maintaining an organization's licence to operate. These are often more powerful messages in the boardroom than damage to credibility and reputation!

A review of the company's present position (if it has one) and its strengths and weaknesses in positioning itself to take a role in shaping the issue will help to give focus for the action planning stage.

The third stage, called rather cumbersomely *issue change*

strategy options, involves making basic decisions about organizational response. The Chase/Jones model cites three options to deal with the change:

reactive change strategy refers to an organization's unwillingness to change with the emphasis on continuing past behaviour, for example, by attempting to postpone the inevitability of public policy decisions. This reluctance to change rarely leaves room for compromise on legislative matters

adaptive change strategy suggests an openness to change and a recognition of its inevitability. This approach relies on planning to anticipate change and offering constructive dialogue to find a form of compromise or accommodation

dynamic response strategy anticipates and attempts to shape the direction of public policy decisions by determining how the campaigning over the issue will be played out. This approach allows the organization to become a leading advocate of change.

After choosing one of these approaches to responding to each issue the organization should decide on policy to support the selected change, which is the fourth stage – *issue action programming.* This requires coordination of resources to provide the maximum support for reaching goals and objectives.

Finally, the requirement for research to evaluate the actual versus intended results of the programme is desirable. We say 'desirable' when it should be 'essential' but, again from practical experience, few companies are willing to do it properly and we have a way to go before enough damning evidence forces better take-up!

It should be remembered that the longer the issue survives, the less choices are available and the more it costs (see Figure 3.3).

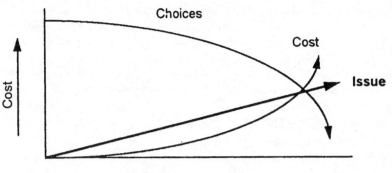

Figure 3.3 *Costs and choices*

Summary

Effective issues management response is based on two key principles: early identification and organized response to influence the public policy process. Issues management is a proactive, anticipatory and planned process designed to influence the development of an issue before it evolves to a stage which requires crisis management. Early action also allows for flexible and creative thinking 'outside the box'.

It is important to remember that issues are constantly being modified and redefined throughout the whole process. Next year's issue is often seeded this year. A brief flurry of media coverage in the UK in 1995 over the potential risk of phthalates – 'gender-bending chemicals' – in infant formula milk preparations, could well herald a period of growing public concern over the impact of these synthetic chemicals on human reproduction and the environment in general. The tobacco industry in the United States provides another example, with the rights of smokers evolving into the rights of non-smokers.

Furthermore, defeat on an issue in one area can be seen as success in another. When tobacco companies had to place a warning label on their products, the *loss* in the legislative arena eventually provided a *win* in the judicial arena because when sued, companies were able to argue that consumers had been warned.

Exerting an influence on the development of identified issues before they bring negative consequences means that an organization should actively represent its interests in the public policy process, by broadening the debate and informing those groups of importance. This *advocacy* participation in the public policy process is central to issues management (Jones & Chase, 1979).

4

An issue ignored is a crisis ensured

Case study: decommissioning the Brent Spar – implications for a global industry

In 1995 Shell UK, a leading oil producer, decided to dispose of the Brent Spar, a redundant North Sea floating storage and tanker loading buoy, in Atlantic deep water. The company undertook and independently commissioned numerous environmental and risk assessment studies, the principal findings of which were released for public consultation. Shell also scrupulously observed all national and international legal and regulatory requirements.

Shell was eventually forced to choose what it and others widely regarded as the second-best environmental option, taking the Spar onshore for break-up, because of intense pressure exerted by Greenpeace and some European governments.

The pressure was not characterized by any significant scientific evidence refuting Shell's case – many leading independent scientific experts supported Shell's recommendations. The consortium of Shell, the operator and Esso, a subsidiary of Exxon, was defeated by a single-issue pressure group which skilfully secured the support of influential politicians and administrators in Europe by shaping public opinion. As a result, the oil industry may face an expensive and environmentally questionable requirement to return all North Sea installations to shore when redundant, contradicting existing international disposal agreements.

The rationale for deep water disposal

The Brent Spar was commissioned in 1976. It is a vertically floating buoy, 141 metres high and fixed to the sea bed. The buoy consists of oil storage tanks at the bottom, capable of holding 300,000 barrels of crude oil, 12 buoyancy tanks towards the middle and a topside containing offshore tanker loading equipment and accommodation for 30 people.

Rising maintenance costs prompted a review in 1991 to conclude that the work necessary to refurbish the facility, to extend its operational life, could cost over £90 million. The buoy would also have to be out of commission for about three years during the work. Given the age of the structure, the presence of a pipeline system for the export of crude oil from the field and the cost of refurbishment, the Spar was taken out of commission in September 1991.

Thirteen methods of abandoning or re-using the Spar were put forward for consideration and six were identified as viable options. These included horizontal or vertical dismantling and onshore disposal, in-field disposal and deep water disposal. Of these, horizontal dismantling and deep water disposal were considered in detail.

The assessments were designed to determine the Best Practicable Environmental Option (BPEO), taking into account factors such as technical feasibility, risks to workforce health and safety, environmental impact, costs and public acceptability. Shell also had to take into account likely additional stress to the structure when upended and the fact that two main storage tanks had been accidentally ruptured some 25 years earlier and repaired only to maintain structural integrity and not on-going use.

In October 1991, undamaged crude oil storage tanks were emptied, process pipe work was flushed through with sea water, buoyancy tanks were emptied, all valves were shut to prevent flooding and loose equipment removed. An analysis showed that an estimated 100 tonnes of oily sludge contained about 9.2 tonnes of oil and a number of heavy metals, with the remainder composed of a mixture of sand and scale. The walls of the storage tanks were, reportedly, coated with an estimated 41.3 tonnes of hydrocarbons in the form of a thin layer of oil and wax. Shell said that scale is commonly found in oil processing facilities and that it may be contaminated by small amounts of naturally occurring radioactive salts from the oil reservoir. The company believed that its impact was minimal with no implications for health or the food chain.

The BPEO demonstrated that the most appropriate action was to dispose of the Spar at an authorized deep water disposal site, as it was the option of least technical risk, minimized workforce exposure to accidents, would have a small but insignificant impact on the environment and was economically the most attractive. Onshore disposal would be a much more technically complex and hazardous operation in safety and occupational health risk terms. Shell summarized its position:

> Extensive studies and an independent report confirmed deep water disposal of the Spar as the simplest operation, posing low risk to health, safety and the environment. It would not be environmentally hazardous and would have a negligible effect on the deep sea environment.

Organizations involved in the 30 studies included the University of Aberdeen, Global Maritime, Metocean, McDermott Engineering, Smith Engineering, Aker, Heerema and Amec.

The decision was taken after consultation with the Scottish Office and other UK government departments, and was endorsed by the UK Department of Trade and Industry. The proposed disposal was in accordance with all relevant UK and international laws and conventions and approvals were received on 17 February 1995.

The Greenpeace allegations

In late May 1995, Shell exchanged correspondence with Green-peace. A letter from Uta Bellion, Chairman of Greenpeace International, addressed to Cor Herkstroter, Chairman of the Committee of Managing Directors of the Royal Dutch/Shell group, commenting on Shell UK's 'appalling plans to dump the Brent Spar', claimed that it was:

> laden with over 100 tonnes of toxic sludge and more than 30 tonnes of radioactive scale. It contains a lethal cocktail including lead, arsenic, mercury, and PCBs which, if allowed to enter the marine environment, would present a considerable threat.

Allegedly, the dumping was 'wholly inconsistent with the best international practice in disposing of oil installations' and that in the Gulf of Mexico, where 'dumping of redundant oil installations is prohibited', Shell practises 'far less environmentally damaging methods of disposal'. Shell UK was charged with showing 'utter contempt' in its treatment of the environment. Greenpeace claimed the credit for publicizing Shell's disposal plans and that the decision to dump the Spar was based on economic, not environmental criteria.

In response, Dr Chris Fay, Chairman and Chief Executive of Shell UK, replying on behalf of Cor Herkstroter, described the 'widely-publicised assertions repeated in your letter' as 'mis-informed and unjustifiably alarmist'. He continued:

> You claim that Shell UK has rejected the best available solution, putting economic performance before the environment, because of the alleged laxity of UK regulatory standards. Neither could be further from the truth.

The UK regulatory regime was amongst the most scrupulous in the world. The letter stated,

> On every count, the procedures, principles and standards which underlie the Brent Spar disposal plan authorised by the British Government represent current best international oil industry practice in respect of the care, rigour and independence of the analysis of the options, the responsible balancing of environ-

mental, safety and health considerations and the extent and openness of consultations with interested parties, including fishermen and environmentalists, which preceded the Government's approval of the disposal plan.

Dr Fay stressed that Shell UK was not predisposed to the offshore disposal of redundant installations simply to save costs. UK government policy, consistent with best international practice, took into account the individual characteristics and circumstances of each disposal on a case-by-case basis. He continued: 'The responsible option in this case, on environmental, safety and health considerations, is carefully managed deep water disposal'. However, he added that the balanced case-by-case approach could lead to onshore recovery and scrapping for many subsequent disposals of redundant British installations.

Shell denied totally that Greenpeace activity had ensured that the disposal plan had become public knowledge, not least because discussions with interested parties had started in 1994. Fay's letter stated:

> We understand that all the governments which are parties to the Oslo Convention governing international standards for the protection of the marine environment were notified months ago of the proposed disposal plan for the Brent Spar.

The Greenpeace comment that Shell UK was prepared to treat the environment with contempt, highlighted the contrast between, as Dr Fay put it, 'those of us who are engaged in the painstaking process of seeking responsible balanced solutions and those, like yourselves, who focus only on the problems'.

The chain reaction begins

The emerging issue of the Brent Spar quickly established a momentum of its own when, on 30 April 1995, Greenpeace activists occupied the Spar amid considerable media interest. In less than a month, from 30 April to 23 May, the UK government had issued a licence for deep water disposal, the German government had lodged a formal protest to its UK counterpart – in spite of making no comment during the earlier compulsory consultation process – and, finally, the activists were removed from the Spar amid one of the most visually striking and intense international broadcast stories of the year. Public interest in this so-called 'David and Goliath' debate, now amplified by a global print and electronic media, quickly brought about top level political resistance as the issue moved cross-border.

At the Esbjerg North Sea Conference in early June, several European countries called for all defunct oil installations to be disposed of onshore, leaving the UK and Norway isolated in arguing for a case-by-case approach.

On 10 June, Shell UK started to tow the Spar to an approved deep Atlantic site – 6000 feet deep and about 150 miles off the west coast of Scotland. At the same time public perception, through widespread editorial fuelled by Greenpeace, was of a location much closer to the mainland with the potential to create enormous environmental damage to the marine ecology.

Public opinion in continental northern Europe became increasingly vociferous in its opposition to Shell's action and by mid-June, eager to demonstrate his green credentials during elections in Germany, Chancellor Kohl protested about the disposal plans to Prime Minister Major at the G7 Summit in Nova Scotia. In a very short period of time a potential issue that was not widely considered to be of particular importance in the UK, had escalated to become one of international public scrutiny and militant action.

In Germany, a boycott of Shell products and picketing of Shell forecourts started and within days some 200 service stations were damaged, with two facilities fire-bombed and one raked with bullets. On 20 June, John Major defended Shell's position on decommissioning the Brent Spar in the House of Commons, only to discover afterwards that in The Hague, the parent company of Shell UK had already decided to abort the decommissioning plan in the face of intense public opposition. As the success of the Greenpeace campaign was acknowledged across the world, Shell was condemned by UK government ministers and the media for its U-turn and the Prime Minister referred to the company as 'wimps'. Michael Heseltine, then UK President of the Board of Trade, said that it was a total embarrassment for Shell and that the company 'should have kept its nerve and done what they believed was right'.

In a press release issued on 20 June, Shell UK effectively confirmed that it was succumbing to pressure. Admitting that the new decision was not taken on a reassessment of the technical factors, the company said that it still believed the deep water disposal of the Brent Spar was the best practicable environmental option.

The *Financial Times* concluded in an editorial on the subject:

> If democracy means the successful exploitation of popular anxieties by a militant minority, then so be it. However, Shell's rout is hardly a victory for rational policy-making, let alone for the environment.

In the aftermath of the Brent Spar incident, commentators have argued that Shell's failure to successfully present its case to a wide audience base not only damaged a reputation for commercial enterprise and environmental vigilence built over many years but created serious financial consequences for the company (for example, through voluntary relinquishment of tax relief) and for the oil industry as a whole if offshore disposal were to be disallowed. The impact of greater public scrutiny, not least surrounding the environmental and social credibility of Shell's operations in Nigeria, has further implications for the business.

Could the surrender have been averted?

The answer has to be 'Yes' and here are our maxims for an effective response.

1. Manage the response

Managing the response to an emerging issue as it gains momentum through the lifecycle curve needs clearly defined roles and responsibilities and the committed time and focused attention of senior management. Without this focus at the absolute top of the organization, reputation and performance are quickly threatened.

In a BBC *Newsnight* interview on 20 June, following Shell's announcement to abandon deep water disposal the interviewer, Jeremy Paxman, challenged Dr Chris Fay over the company's management competence in handling the issue and argued that a company shouldn't fail with the full might of government behind it. In response Dr Fay said: 'Am I expected to react every day to the misinformation that the media takes in and spend all my time arguing against that misinformation while the media doesn't seem to want to take hold of the total story?' Clearly, responding to every potential issue isn't feasible nor is it good management practice. However, when key issues do emerge, it is critical for the chief executive to decide at the earliest possible stage when to get directly involved and what resources need to be allocated to manage the task. In the case of Brent Spar, the chief executive did not make these decisions early enough.

> *Because of the consequences of failing to manage and respond to public opinion, senior management must have appropriate systems and resources in place to be able to focus – full-time if necessary – on the management of the issue.*

2. Understand the public view

The increasing demands of public scrutiny place new pressures on organizations to be alert, aware and ready to shape or respond to potential public debate. It is often about harnessing and managing emotion.

Shell assumed that because it had followed all the international regulatory agreements and had secured the cooperation of the British and other governments (at least initially) there was no need to seek approval from a wider audience. Indeed, Dr Fay quite reasonably stated that it was 'the first example where governments have openly protested against an option which has been carried out in a lawful and proper manner'.

> *The speed and amplification techniques of a modern, global media and the growth and sophistication of single-issue campaign groups*

make them extremely capable in reaching and relating to public emotion. These factors create a new imperative for institutions and corporations to monitor and assess public perception and behaviour on any matter that could affect, either directly or indirectly, operational performance.

3. Make the case – clear and simple

Shell had difficulty explaining detailed scientific analysis succinctly, meaningfully and swifty. By the time that some allegations were refuted more were made. In contrast, images of Greenpeace members aboard the Brent Spar being attacked by plumes of water fired from nearby vessels, made instant news and more interesting broadcast viewing than scientific experts 'dryly' assessing the merits of the proposed decommissioning plan.

As we described in Chapter 1, there is growing evidence of the public's ability to challenge reassurances about risk made by government and industry. Reliance solely on the availability of scientific or technical data without communicating clear messages that distil key findings in a manner that responds to potential public concern about a particular risk is simply not enough to prevent or win the debate. Furthermore, research into memory loss indicates that we forget two-thirds of what we absorb in a day and 98 per cent in a month. Clear message points repeated over time help to make sense of complex issues for most of us.

The avoidance of complex language and statistics is essential. Instead, the use of analogies to emphasize the low degree of potential risk to the environment, coupled with basic facts, message points and illustrations are effective mechanisms for making a clear and compelling case. This approach can be used, for example, to demonstrate the remoteness and depth of the disposal location, the potential for marine life to colonize the structure over time and the health and safety benefits of offshore disposal.

This type of approach isn't about talking down to people but it is about focusing on a few key points, and constantly and consistently communicating those points to secure understanding and, ultimately, support from the majority of those either interested or directly involved.

4. Find out who you are up against and how they are likely to behave

Shell appeared to have no knowledge of the planned campaign by Greenpeace and was seemingly taken by surprise when correspondence started to fly and activists attempted to occupy the Spar.

> The whole point of an early warning system is to monitor, anticipate and assess the likely origin and evolution of potential issues. This involves gathering information on the agendas and activities of **all** relevant audiences, however peripheral in the beginning. In the case of issues relating to public health, safety and environmental protection it is essential that organizations pay particular attention to special interest groups. Building a profile of the working methods and organization of such groups through examining the characteristics, style and approach to campaigning, membership recruitment, funding, promotional activities and current agenda setting, will provide valuable intelligence for planning purposes.

5. Work with the media

Shell seemed unable to counter the powerful visual icons offered by a very media-aware, single issue pressure group. Conveying detailed environmental analysis in a 'sound bite' context is a tough challenge but possible to do through some of the techniques described earlier. This needs to be coupled with a clear understanding of the working practices and demands of the media. Shell failed to make this distinction and put its faith in sound science rather than sound bites. There was a clear opportunity to communicate the low potential risk of offshore disposal, the complexity in health and safety terms of onshore disposal and the fact that, for example, many of the heavy metals contained in the Spar are produced in much higher volumes by nature.

Shell was not slow to disseminate material to the media but the latter showed little sustained interest in the story until Greenpeace first occupied the Spar on 30 April. It is inevitable that because of our increasing scepticism and lack of trust in big things, ie corporations and institutions, sections of the media may be biased in favour of campaign groups. In particular, the concept of a 'David and Goliath' combat provides mouth-watering potential for sensational editorial. There is also a tendency by the media to call for and critically scrutinize a company's arguments and supporting data to a much greater degree than that of a pressure group.

Some analysts criticized Shell for not taking a more positive stance with the media earlier. However, the company could argue with some justification that seeking a higher profile may have attracted disproportionate attention to a complex issue. The right balance is often difficult to determine until it is too late.

Finally, as the issue was developing, a perception evolved that Shell representatives were seldom seen or heard on radio or television. Producers turned to other 'experts' which helped to inject some independence into the story but implied, however unjustly, that Shell was keeping a low profile.

The need for regular availability of no more than two or three designated spokespeople for communication with the media is essential.

6. Sing from the same hymn sheet

Faced with managing an issue, a company must never appear divided. *Perceptions matter.* The perception was that Shell did not speak with one voice. When public outrage developed in Germany, the local company attempted to distance itself from its UK counterpart, claiming that it had no influence there. One comment attributed to the German chief executive was that the first he knew about the proposed deep water disposal plan was when he saw the Brent Spar on television! Later, according to a press report, Shell Germany apologized to the public for paying more attention to scientists and authorities than to customers' wishes.

Similarly, Shell in The Netherlands did not want to be seen supporting London, and a senior Shell executive in Austria was quoted as saying that the sinking of the Brent Spar was intolerable.

Although sometimes difficult to institute across international and highly decentralized organization structures, it is imperative that policy guidelines are introduced and adhered to in such a way that there is always a single, consistently communicated position on an issue, with authorized spokespeople assigned to represent that position.

7. Remember – issues transcend borders and politics

Issues that involve an international industry and regulatory environment rarely stay local. Transmission of information and opinion through a host of newly available electronic media cannot be geographically constrained.

Similarly, changing political systems and agendas demand constant review and assessment no matter how removed from equivalent national institutions. Shell in London acknowledged that it was astonished by the depth of German feeling on environmental issues relating to oceans. Why? Any international organization should be tuned into policy-making in all the markets in which it operates, particularly in those that could be affected by a potential change or development like the Brent Spar.

This also applies to monitoring the methods of working and campaign activities of special interest groups. Shell decided that it would not discuss issues with Greenpeace until the illegal occupation of the Spar was ended. However reasonable such a stance may have been, it was a turning point.

Talking to an organization may give it added status, but it can help to publicly demonstrate a commitment to listen and potentially negotiate a resolution of conflict.

Appropriate early warning systems and internal information networks, which can operate across borders, are essential ingredients to the effective strategic planning and issues management functions within the organization.

Conclusion

The *Financial Times* noted:

In hindsight, Shell failed to detect the extent of public concern in

continental Europe or to win adequate support for its argument
that the best place for the Brent Spar was in a deep trench in the
Atlantic. As a result, years of careful cultivation by Shell of an
environmentally friendly image have been thrown away.

It is always easy to criticize corporate response with the benefit
of hindsight and it is important to note how rigorously Shell
followed every procedure with regard to agreed international
regulatory policy and environmental best practice.

Shell, alongside other large companies, could be forgiven for
questioning the validity of international agreements sponsored
in the framework of the law. If governments accept the rules,
ignore the deadline for comment on projects devised in strict
accordance with the requirements and then reverse their stance
because of local protest, where does that place the credibility of
such agreements?

Ruminating on the consequences of Shell's decision to do a
U-turn on the planned disposal, Shell UK's director of public
affairs wrote:

> Businesses will now have to include in their planning not just the
> views and rational arguments of all concerned – whether
> opponents or supporters – but will also have to come to grips
> with an area of deep seated emotions, subconscious instincts and
> symbolic gestures.

The Brent Spar issue is summarized in Figure 4.1.

POTENTIAL ISSUE
- Brent Spar decommissioned — Sept '91
- Abandonment studies commence — Oct '91
- Shell begins discussing disposal with regulatory authorities — Sept '92
- Aberdeen University study endorses deepwater disposal — Feb '94
- External consultation — Feb '94
- 'Best Practicable Environmental Option' and 'Impact Hypothesis' to DTI — Oct '94

CURRENT ISSUE
- Top level resistance escalates and moves across border:
  - Esbjerg North Sea Conference – calls for all oil installations to be disposed of on land — 8–9 June '95
  - Shell UK tows Spar to deep Atlantic disposal site — 10 Jun '95
  - Northern European public opinion strongly opposed
  - Chancellor Kohl protests about disposal at G7 Summit — 15–17 Jun '95

DORMANT ISSUE
- Consequences
  - Shell UK reputation badly damaged; bottom-line impact following product boycott
  - Voluntary relinquishment of tax relief (est. £11 million)
  - Huge cost to industry if offshore disposal disallowed (Brent Spar cost of onshore disposal £46m; cost offshore £11m)

EMERGING ISSUE
- Government announces intention to approve deepwater disposal; notifies relevant European governments — Feb '95
- Debate enters wider public domain
  - Greenpeace activists occupy Spar — 30 Apr '95
  - Govt issues disposal licence — 9 May '95
  - German govt lodges protest — 23 May '95
  - Activists removed from Spar; heavy television coverage

CRISIS ISSUE
- German boycott and picketing of Shell forecourts begins — 15 Jun '95
- Protesters in Germany threaten/attack Shell service stations — 15–20 Jun '95
- Prime Minister defends Shell in House of Commons
- Shell aborts operation and makes public announcement; fails to inform PM before House of Commons speech — 20 Jun '95
- Shell UK referred to as 'wimps' by PM; U-turn condemned by broadsheets

Figure 4.1 *Shell UK – Brent Spar*

Case study: mad cows and Englishmen – the story of BSE

Introduction

The only simple factors in the mad cow disease drama were the initials BSE and CJD. The existence of a probable link between bovine spongiform encephalopathy (BSE) and Creutzfeldt-Jakob disease (CJD), a rare and fatal brain disease in humans, was revealed in March 1996. CJD has an incubation period of between 10 and 50 years and the average age of its victims had been 63. Researchers in Edinburgh, however, identified a new variant whose victims had an average age of 27. It seemed likely that BSE had crossed species to affect man.

It was clear that some cattle would have to be slaughtered and burned to prevent infected meat from entering the human food chain. But confusion reigned. There was no agreement on how many cattle should be culled, whether this should include animals less than 30 months old, who should compensate farmers, and the magnitude of the potential human epidemic. One scientist claimed Britain could face up to 500,000 cases of CJD. Others thought the risks were minimal, although there have been 14 deaths from the new variant of CJD since it was discovered. Some experts said BSE would be eradicated within two years, others suggested it was endemic.

Relations with Brussels, none too cordial at the best of times, were further soured by EU bans on British beef and bickering over the size of the cull. Beef sales in Britain recovered after the initial panic, but remained sharply lower on the Continent. The number of slaughtered cattle at the end of 1996 was well over 1,000,000, with no end to the ban in sight. BSE was caused by feeding these herbivores with animal protein from sheep suffering from scrapie; CJD has been a reminder, in an age of genetic engineering, of the unpleasant way in which nature can respond to human experiments.

How scientific information was assessed and communicated by politicians and the media to an increasingly anxious public and responded to by a major industry potentially on the verge of financial ruin represent the ingredients for one of the most complex food issues facing the UK in recent times.

The story unfolds...

The beginning of the BSE crisis can be traced back to the 1970s, following changes made to the processing of sheep offal into cattle feed, designed to make meat and bone meal more appetizing.

In September 1979, the British government received a warning from the Royal Commission concerning the dangers of passing animal diseases to humans via infected foodstuffs. This was followed by advice from the Institute for Animal Science and Health in The Netherlands, that meat rendering at low temperatures could have dangerous implications for the spread of disease across species barriers. Unlike their British counterparts, British renderers had, in some cases, used temperatures lower than 100°C, thus increasing the risk of infection.

BSE was officially diagnosed by the UK Central Veterinary Laboratory in November 1986. The findings were not made public until 5 June of the following year when the Chief Veterinary Officer (CVO) informed government ministers of the disease. Studies commissioned to identify possible causes of the disease concluded in December 1987 that cattle feed made from meat and bone meal was the only viable cause of BSE. Papers published in scientific journals over the following months began to raise concerns over the potential impact of BSE on human health.

As soon as other European countries suspected that animal meal could be the source of the disease, its use was banned, with France and Ireland taking the added precaution of destroying all animals in any herd with a case of BSE.

In July 1988, six months after the cause of the disease had been identified, the British government ordered a ban on the use of scrapie-infected sheep offals from cattle feed. This was followed in August by legislation requiring the slaughter of all

BSE-infected animals and the destruction of their milk. A compensation scheme was introduced providing farmers with 50 per cent of the market value of each infected cow.

Faced with an uncertain and potentially catastrophic financial future, it is alleged that some farmers marketed cows with early signs of BSE and continued to use old cattle feed in the absence of rigorous monitoring of the bans. It was not until seven months later that the government increased compensation to 100 per cent, to prevent further infected meat entering the human food chain.

In May 1989, Dr Hugh Fraser, a leading scientist at the Institute of Animal Health carrying out government experiments on BSE, was interviewed on BBC Radio 4's *Face the Facts* programme. He said; 'there are suspect tissues from certain categories of cattle which it would be prudent, I think, to remove from human consumption' and identified pies and pâtés as sources of suspect tissues most likely to carry the disease. Following his interview, the Ministry of Agriculture instructed scientists at the Institute not to talk to the media about BSE.

The calm before the storm

In November 1989, the government announced a ban on the use of certain specified bovine offals (SBOs) thought most likely to carry BSE. This action was explained as a precautionary measure, but designed to maintain consumer confidence in British beef. The working party on BSE, established by the government in 1988 to investigate possible human implications of the disease, concluded the following year that it seemed unlikely that BSE could cross the species barrier. The possibility of a 'species jump', however, could not be ruled out – the implications of which would be 'extremely serious'. Despite doubt among members of the scientific community, the CVO said on national television, 'We don't believe there are any implications [from BSE] for humans at this time'.

As early as February 1990, however, the Institute of Environmental Health Officers submitted a report to the Ministry of Agriculture outlining problems with the implementation of the offals ban. Abattoirs were not rigorously enforcing the new restrictions and SBOs were still getting into the human food chain. The Ministry did not respond to the report.

In September 1990, renewed fears about the ability of BSE to 'jump species' were caused by the announcement that a laboratory transmission had caused the disease to develop in a pig. The then agriculture minister, John Gummer, responded to negative media comment with a photo-call depicting himself and his 4-year-old daughter eating beefburgers made with British beef. In a subsequent television interview, Gummer stated that his priority was first and foremost to 'make sure the public knows that it is perfectly safe to eat British beef'.

In 1991, reports in the national media about the possible spread of BSE reached new levels following the discovery that a domestic cat had died from the disease. The cat's death was assumed to have been caused by eating pet food made with infected offals, prior to the 1988 voluntary ban on the use of SBOs by major pet food manufacturers. The CVO dismissed the incident by saying 'this is only one cat death out of seven million cats in the UK and there is no reason for cause for concern at all'.

1991 also saw the first evidence that the Government's feed ban was not working with the announcement of the first case of BSE in cattle offspring born after the ban was implemented.

Debate over the dangers to humans continued with the government issuing countless assurances that British beef was safe despite growing doubt among the scientific community. In October 1992, as reports of BSE continued to increase, the CVO again appeared on national television to say: 'there is no need to be alarmed and so far as the public is concerned, there is no risk at all from consuming beef in this country'.

The issue rumbled on over the next three years as unannounced checks on abattoirs began to highlight failings in the implementation of the offals ban. With the absence of new findings or government initiatives, media and public interest began to decline.

1995 saw the issue ratchet up the lifecycle curve at alarming speed:

- In September, new evidence demonstrated a possible link between BSE and the rare human brain disease, Creutzfeldt-Jakob disease (CJD). James Ironside, an experienced neuropathologist at the Western General Hospital in Edinburgh, discovered a new variant of CJD that had recently caused the death of two young people. There were significant differences in the formation of this strain of the disease and a more familiar type of CJD traditionally only found in older people. Ironside believed his discovery could somehow be linked to BSE.
- In October, *The Sunday Times* reported that more than one million infected cattle may have entered the food chain.
- At the end of November, Sir Bernard Tomlinson, another eminent neuropathologist, stated that he would not be eating burgers, pies and other processed meats due to uncertainty over whether BSE could be transmitted to humans.

A case of too little too late

The government embarked on a damage limitation exercise as hundreds of schools began to take beef off their menus and beef sales fell by 25 per cent. British Agriculture Minister, Douglas Hogg, stated, 'British beef has never been safer', arguing that safety measures imposed by the government had prevented any infected meat entering the food chain. But confusion arose when he simultaneously extended the existing offal ban to include food from the spinal cord and mechanically recovered meat, immediately raising concerns that the existing ban had not been adequate.

Even in a December television interview, the Health Minister, Stephen Dorrell, persisted: 'Science suggests that there isn't a link and secondly, even if science was wrong on that subject, we've removed from the human food chain the organs that could conceivably be linked to a transmission'.

By the end of 1995, the CJD surveillance unit had examined the brains of six young people whose death had been caused by the new strain of CJD; the number of deaths rose to eight by the end of the following February.

An urgent briefing was arranged on 8 March to communicate the findings of the surveillance unit to members of the spongiform encephalopathy advisory committee (SEAC). Two weeks later a ninth case of new variant CJD was discovered. The CMO and CVO were immediately informed. Discovery of a tenth case within days led scientists to believe that exposure to BSE was the most likely cause.

On 19 March, the British Prime Minister called a crisis cabinet meeting after being informed that leading scientists believed exposure to BSE may cause CJD in humans, thus challenging a decade of government reassurances about the safety of beef.

The potential financial implications for the UK economy were daunting – the prospect of having to destroy Britain's 12 million cattle was estimated as costing between £10 and 20 billion. The outlook for the beef and associated processing industries was devastating with the potential for businesses failing, significant job losses and a host of other major economic, political and social implications.

The following day, the Health Minister announced to the House of Commons that new scientific evidence relating to recent cases of CJD in young people indicated BSE might be transmissible to humans: 'The [spongiform encephalopathy advisory] committee have concluded that the most likely explanation at present is that these cases are linked to exposure to BSE before the introduction of the Specified Bovine Offals ban in 1989.'

The government pledged commitment to take on board the advice from SEAC and other leading scientists, and stated that original controls on the slaughter and processing of beef introduced in 1988 would be tightened and rigorously monitored. The Health Minister stressed the risk of contracting the disease remained 'extremely low'. By this time, however, intense media speculation over the risks of a human epidemic fuelled public anxiety further; editorials stated that the government's handling of the beef crisis was characterized by 'dither and delay'.

France was the first country to react, introducing a total ban on British beef imports, worth £220 million, and was quickly joined by other European countries. Thousands more British schools took beef off the menu and sales prices plummeted. The European Union endorsed a worldwide ban on exports of British beef on 27 March.

At the same time, many restaurants, including major fast food chains, removed all beef dishes from their menus. McDonalds took out full page advertisements in the national media informing the public that the company was using alternative sources to British beef.

In an attempt to calm the panic over BSE, the Ministry of Agriculture announced that all British cattle over 30 months old would be destroyed at the end of their productive lives, reducing the risk of infected meat entering the food chain. But because the disease had been seen in animals younger than 30 months, the policy was widely criticized by EU members, the media and the public, as a costly half-measure that did not remove the risk of BSE entering the food chain.

The crisis rapidly became political following the EU ban, with the British government criticizing the EU for its 'knee-jerk' reaction which further undermined consumer confidence. In retaliation, the Prime Minister announced, on 21 May 1996, that Britain would embark on a policy of non-cooperation with the EU, effectively freezing certain legislative procedures until agreement over the criteria needed to lift the ban could be reached. The EU remained unimpressed; member states were far more concerned about protecting their own beef markets which had seen a 25 per cent drop in demand. The Agriculture Commission pledged financial support in the form of compensation to British farmers as a gesture to help resolve the crisis. By the end of August 1996, the EU and UK governments had invested £2.65 billion in propping up the European beef industry.

Regardless of compensation, the financial and emotional impact on farmers, meat processors and butchers throughout the UK soon became apparent. Charles Runge, chief executive of the Royal Agricultural Society of England explained the panic: 'A lot of people who have contacted me are not so much angry as bloody frightened. They see their livelihoods being taken away from them for reasons they don't understand'.

The cull set in motion by the government became a source of constant media criticism highlighting the complex logistical problems that were already posing enormous difficulties for destruction and disposal of carcasses. Questions remained over the real effectiveness of the slaughter programme. Some experts claimed it was 'too little too late', bearing in mind the potentially long incubation period before symptoms of the disease were identified and ongoing uncertainty over the risks of BSE crossing species barriers. In May, *The Sunday Telegraph* argued; 'this chaotically ill-organised plan to incinerate all cattle over 30 months old flies in the face of all scientific advice' and suggested that to cull those herds known to be infected with BSE would have been a far more sensible option.

Additional legislation introduced in August 1996 attempted to demonstrate a tightening of the defence against the spread of BSE by making possession of animal feeds made partly from farm animals a criminal offence. Media interest began to wane from the early summer and sales recovered, with British beef reappearing on supermarket shelves.

The EU, nevertheless, remained adamant that the ban on imports from the UK could not be lifted until the cull was widened. New scientific evidence indicated that BSE could pass from mother to calf, highlighting the need for a much more comprehensive slaughter programme.

By November 1996, 14 cases of the new variant of CJD had been confirmed. Nearly one million animals had been slaughtered at an estimated cost in compensation of £460 million. The Treasury estimated that the total cost of the slaughter would be £2.3 billion over the next two years.

While latest research indicated the likelihood of a CJD epidemic was remote and that BSE would have almost run its course by 2001 regardless of the cull, scientists acknowledged that it would be at least eight to ten years before clear evidence on the risks of BSE was known; a cure for CJD would take much longer.

Our verdict

As we explained in Chapter 1, communicating about risk has special requirements.

With scientific evidence about the risk of contracting CJD from BSE so unclear, it has not been easy for government ministers to tread the narrow line between complacency and alarmism. In retrospect, however, the government committed a number of basic mistakes, which could have been avoided early in the issue lifecycle.

1. A stitch in time
Unlike its European counterparts, the British government failed to impose and monitor controls as soon as BSE had been identified. It was unforgivably slow to respond in identifying and slaughtering sick cows and to pursue the causes of the outbreak more rigorously.

2. Half-measures won't work
It was a mistake early on to pay farmers only half the market price for infected cattle. There were persistent rumours of farmers rushing cattle suspected of having BSE to slaughter-houses rather than settling for half-payment.

3. Start as you mean to go on
The government's repeated tightening of controls on the beef industry over the last ten years to try and ensure that infected beef did not reach consumers implies that it would have been more prudent to impose stricter controls right from the beginning. By 1996, BSE had killed 160,000 cattle on more than 32,000 farms and that figure had risen to 1,000,000 at year end.

4. A clear strategy avoids knee-jerk penalties later
More thought should have been given by policy makers to defining a clear strategy before announcing in March 1996 that the possibility of a link with human brain disease seemed greater than had first been thought. The government should not have

sprung that announcement as a surprise on its bemused European partners. By denying that neighbouring countries should have a right to act to protect their own beef industries, significant negative feeling developed across the EU towards the UK.

5. Don't assume the public is ignorant

The biggest error was one of communication. Government ministers insisted, over and over again, that there was absolutely no risk to human health from BSE. While there was no certainty either way, such confident reassurance was imprudent and, subsequently, compounded public cynicism and anxiety. The stunt in 1992 by John Gummer, then agriculture minister, of feeding a beefburger (unsuccessfully) to his 4-year-old daughter in front of television cameras, now looks ludicrous.

6. Act swiftly, decisively and responsibly

While elected governments have a duty to represent the best interests of a diverse electorate, including industries which play an important role in providing products and services to consumers, in matters of public health, those same governments must demonstrate an ability to act swiftly and decisively to protect the public from both real and perceived risk.

7. Politics shouldn't come before public health (but what's new!)

A combination of threats from Brussels, restless backbenchers and panicky headlines led the government to make policy decisions driven by pressure and panic, for example:

- the decision to cull cows over 30 months old, together with a further 147,000 under that age but deemed to be at risk, when research findings published in 1996 indicated that such action would have no tangible effect on the eradication of BSE
- the attempt to shift blame to the EU for introducing and maintaining a ban on British beef, by retaliating with a policy of non-cooperation on inter-governmental decision-making.

8. Find credible, independent and trustworthy spokespeople
A key lesson from this and other public health risk issues over the years relates to the need for government institutions to establish a method for delivering scientific information to the public untainted by the suspicion of political or commercial calculations. Any links between government departments, which normally represent the interests of farmers and other producers, and advice to consumers should be removed.

As far as possible, scientific advice on health and safety issues should be communicated to consumers by scientists, capable of distilling complex data in clear risk/benefit terms, and not by politicians.

The BSE issue is summarized in Figure 4.2.

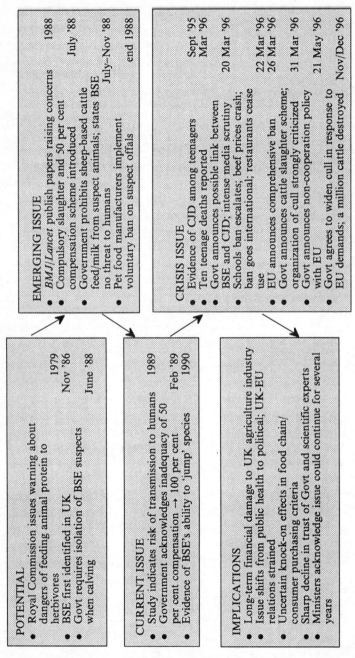

POTENTIAL
- Royal Commission issues warning about dangers of feeding animal protein to herbivores — 1979
- BSE first identified in UK — Nov '86
- Govt requires isolation of BSE suspects when calving — June '88

CURRENT ISSUE
- Study indicates risk of transmission to humans — 1989
- Government acknowledges inadequacy of 50 per cent compensation → 100 per cent — Feb '89
- Evidence of BSE's ability to 'jump' species — 1990

IMPLICATIONS
- Long-term financial damage to UK agriculture industry
- Issue shifts from public health to political; UK-EU relations strained
- Uncertain knock-on effects in food chain/consumer purchasing criteria
- Sharp decline in trust of Govt and scientific experts
- Ministers acknowledge issue could continue for several years

EMERGING ISSUE
- *BMJ/Lancet* publish papers raising concerns — 1988
- Compulsory slaughter and 50 per cent compensation scheme introduced — July '88
- Government prohibits sheep-based cattle feed/milk from suspect animals; states BSE no threat to humans — July–Nov '88
- Pet food manufacturers implement voluntary ban on suspect offals — end 1988

CRISIS ISSUE
- Evidence of CJD among teenagers — Sept '95
- Ten teenage deaths reported — Mar '96
- Govt announces possible link between BSE and CJD; intense media scrutiny — 20 Mar '96
- Schools ban escalates; beef prices crash; ban goes international; restaurants cease use — 22 Mar '96
- EU announces comprehensive ban — 26 Mar '96
- Govt announces cattle slaughter scheme; organization of cull strongly criticized — 31 Mar '96
- Govt announces non-cooperation policy with EU — 21 May '96
- Govt agrees to widen cull in response to EU demands; a million cattle destroyed — Nov/Dec '96

Figure 4.2 *BSE*

Case study: CFCs – finding an essential breathing space

Seventy million patients throughout the world rely on medicines delivered by a metered dose inhaler (MDI) to treat their asthma and other respiratory diseases. Few have been aware that their pocket-sized delivery system remains one of the last sources of chlorofluorocarbons (CFCs) escaping into the atmosphere and contributing to the depletion of the ozone layer.

In 1987, an international agreement was reached under the auspices of the United Nations Environment Programme, which called for a freeze on production of selected CFCs and for all signatories to begin to phase out their use.

Industries using CFCs were presented with a legislative framework which would eventually lead to total ban and significant financial implications associated with current and future manufacturing processes.

A group of leading pharmaceutical companies affected by these changes decided to act in concert to minimise risks to commercial performance and potential public criticism. The issues centred on the industry's ability to respond to the new regulations in order to help protect the environment, while at the same time ensuring continued and safe supply of asthma medication throughout the world. The consortium's programme of work continues but this case study illustrates how industry can successfully handle complex issues to the benefit of a wide range of audiences.

The background

CFCs are man-made substances and were developed by General Motors in the 1920s for use as coolants in automotive air conditioning systems. Because CFCs have many useful properties and are non-toxic to humans, industry quickly found multiple uses for them – in refrigeration, air conditioning, foam blowing, aerosol propellants and technical cleaning solutions.

In 1974, however, an American scientist predicted that it was possible for CFCs to destroy the ozone layer. In the absence of firm evidence, governments were slow to respond until in 1977 the US administration introduced a ban on non-essential aerosols. Western European countries responded with a voluntary 30 per cent reduction in aerosol CFCs and, in some countries, a ban on most aerosol uses was introduced. In spite of growing pressure from special interest groups, public policy makers did not consider concerted legislative action was necessarily based solely on scientific theory.

By 1985 all the proof that was needed emerged through dramatic satellite pictures that revealed a white hole over the South Pole. The discovery by a British scientist provided a focus for debate and study across the world and quickly generated public interest.

Scientists gathered conclusive evidence of the link between CFCs and ozone depletion and started to predict how cumulative use would affect the atmosphere.

At a time of growing interest in environmental issues, the media amplified scientific and special interest group arguments about the need for atmospheric protection. This helped to create an emerging issue of importance for public debate and potential public policy formulation.

The emergence of this new risk issue posed serious questions for environmental and health policy. If the protective ozone layer was reduced further, greater levels of ultra-violet radiation would reach the Earth's surface causing increased risk of cancer and potential ecological imbalance – and on a global basis. The question was no longer *should* CFCs be banned but *when* and *how*.

The United Nations provided an umbrella organization to bring national governments together to decide on a course of action. Under the terms of the 1987 Montreal Protocol on Substances that Deplete the Ozone Layer, all CFC production except for designated essential uses was to be phased out throughout the developed world.

Concern focused primarily on large industrial uses of CFC compounds in refrigeration, air conditioning and foam manufacture. However, the implications of the agreement were also profound for the pharmaceutical industry.

Over the last three decades, CFC emissions from MDIs have amounted to less than 1 per cent of the total and these inhaler devices provide probably the safest and most effective delivery system for treating millions of asthma sufferers worldwide. However, each inhaler contains about 15 grams of CFC – enough to destroy one tonne of ozone, the equivalent needed to protect about 1,600 square metres of the Earth's surface. Without these devices millions of people suffering from respiratory disease would be affected, but with them, the long-term impact on the Earth's atmosphere could be significant.

To the pharmaceutical industry, the medical and commercial imperatives presented by CFC phase-out were clear:

- the total worldwide market for asthma medicines is worth several billion pounds; a substantial percentage of this involves the regular use of MDIs
- if CFCs were to go, alternative propellants had to be found
- if a new propellant could be found for asthma inhalers, switching patients to a new inhaler could not happen overnight; the logistics of replacing 450 million devices used each year would be enormous
- significant financial, medical and social differences existed between managing the potential change in developed as opposed to developing countries
- many patients would be reluctant to change from a tried and tested device they depended on for treating a life-threatening disease
- most patients and doctors were unaware that CFCs were used in asthma inhalers
- explaining that the use of CFCs in inhalers was safe while acknowledging that the same CFCs were responsible for destroying the ozone layer would not be easy.

While it was inconceivable that the Protocol would deny patients access to the use of inhalers without an appropriate alternative, the pharmaceutical industry was now facing the fact that by the late 1990s, the use of CFCs would be completely phased out.

The industry had to recognize and accept the environmental realities. The need for change was clear and so the pharmaceutical companies involved in asthma treatment agreed that they needed to be a partner in the change process.

How action planning got underway

Nine major companies agreed to act together and formed The International Pharmaceutical Aerosol Consortium – IPAC. The priorities for IPAC were to:

- communicate the industry's commitment to change
- inform influencers and decision makers about the risks of asthma
- ensure the Montreal Protocol's Technology and Economic Assessment Panel (TEAC) agreed with the industry consensus that the preferred method of drug administration for treatment of asthma is by the use of inhalers
- find a candidate for a replacement propellant, test it for medical use and seek regulatory approval for market introduction as soon as possible
- make representations to public policy makers to secure essential use exemption for MDIs, while reformulated products were developed, tested and brought to market
- agree an appropriate strategy for an orderly transition process for replacement products to minimize public health risks.

The IPAC consortium approach offered benefits both to member companies and to Protocol coordinators. Working in unison would help to speed the whole process of developing an approved replacement for CFCs. Participants would pool research and development expertise and resources, as well as share the considerable costs. In addition, the consortium created one voice for the industry – vital for success in putting forward a coherent and valid case to the many groups participating in such a complex, unfolding debate.

However, there were also a number of potential barriers for the consortium, namely:

- lack of informed knowledge about the importance of medical inhalers
- country-by-country competition to lead the race to totally phase out CFCs would require national legislation to ensure an exemption clause
- special interest groups were likely to campaign aggressively for a 'no exemptions' outcome
- recycling CFCs, an option favoured by some groups, could run the risk of contamination; support for this process had to be countered
- the proliferation and complexity of other related legislation would make the communication process particularly challenging.

Defining a potential solution

The first step was to establish a representative task force with clear guidelines on methods of working, roles and responsibilities, and resource allocation. Importantly, a secretariat was established employing an environmental law firm and administrative support to ensure rigorous coordination and implementation of agreed actions.

A network of working groups was established on a geographic and institutional basis for information gathering, analysis, response strategy coordination and implementation. This framework was essential to ensure organized, informed and targeted communication; to reduce duplication of effort; and to track, target and mobilize important groups (scientific, environmental, medical, special interest and other influencers and policy makers) at UN, EU, member state and regional levels.

The principal focus of IPAC's work had to be finding a suitable replacement and gaining regulatory approval. Without this all other activity would be pointless. Two sub-committees were set up to investigate alternatives to CFCs – HFA-134a and HFA-227. Pre-competitive cooperation on research and development was agreed.

It was essential for patient welfare, however, that in the rush to resolve the CFC problem, policy makers did not inadvertently ban essential medical uses. Research conducted by IPAC members among doctor and patients groups indicated only a 20 per cent awareness that asthma inhalers contained CFCs. The same research showed that awareness was even lower among the decision makers who would actually shape the policies designed to phase out CFCs. So there was a real danger that a crucial life-saving device could be overlooked in the complex policy formulation process.

On the basis that it takes up to ten years to test, validate and gain approval for a new medical treatment, IPAC realized that a CFC-free inhaler would not be ready to beat the deadline. Even if one were available sooner, the low level of awareness of the issue would make it virtually impossible to switch all patients to the new inhaler in such a short timeframe.

IPAC was faced with two options: convince the policy makers to extend the deadline for CFC phase-out, or make the case for an exemption for essential CFC uses for which there is currently no viable alternative.

As environmental issues were high on the public policy agenda in developed countries during the pre-recessionary period of the mid/late 1980s and given that the threat to the ozone layer had been scientifically proven and was the subject of widespread concern, the second option was chosen as the consortium's position. Once IPAC had agreed this course of action, a clear strategy and action plan was required to secure the exemption.

Getting the issues management programme underway

All relevant decision makers and influencer groups needed to be made aware of the issues at stake and understand that:

- asthma affects 70 million people worldwide and is a life-threatening disease for which there is no cure; patient care must be protected
- IPAC supports the environmental objectives of the Protocol
- IPAC is working to a non-CFC inhaler solution
- the non-CFC alternative will take time to develop

- an exemption is therefore required for certain medical uses of CFCs
- limited quantities of CFCs must be available for this purpose.

The Protocol was being negotiated with all member countries of the United Nations. Within each country a wide range of people had to be reached, not just the decision makers but also those responsible for advising on and drafting environmental, scientific and healthcare policy. Because of IPAC's medical case, it was essential that government health departments, medical opinion leaders, doctor and patient support groups understood the implications. It was also important that they could be mobilized to actively support the consortium's case in the face of critical opinion from special interest groups, parts of the media, competitors and other industries with vested interests.

Messages were agreed and tested by IPAC centrally. They were kept simple and to the point. It was important that IPAC was not perceived to be objecting to the central tenant of the Protocol – the need to protect the ozone layer. It was also crucial that the industry was not seen to be dragging its feet or being self-serving at the expense of patient welfare.

To support IPAC member companies in their contact programmes, a comprehensive package of written and visual materials was produced designed to address as many audiences as possible with minimal adaptation by audience and country. A key document and positioning statement, titled *An Essential Breathing Space for Patients*, presented a clear and concise version of the case for an exemption.

External lobbying and issue management specialists were employed. The secretariat advised on presenting case materials to the committees of the Montreal Protocol and to coordinate, track and evaluate consortium activities and their impact as the programme evolved. This provided invaluable information for refining and focusing communication in such a way that opinion could be influenced so that necessary behavioural changes happened. In-country working groups of member company and consultancy staff reported on a regular basis to the secretariat. They were responsible for highlighting key developments, both positive and negative, and seeking input on successful programming in other geographic and institutional areas.

One working group was given responsibility for overseeing the activities of the various technical, scientific and legal committees established by UNEP. Another working group coordinated all contact with the European Union. Other groups targeted in-country communication with particular emphasis on mobilizing as much independent third-party support as possible.

The use of a hub-and-spoke organizational structure with a strong central focus for policy formulation and review in the secretariat helped to minimize bureaucracy. The use of electronic document management was also an important time-saver.

The Consortium was, ultimately, successful in achieving its initial objectives. An exemption was won for the continued use of CFCs beyond the general deadline of the Montreal Protocol. In addition, European Union regulatory approval was received to develop an HFA-134a-based propellant.

More recently, IPAC has submitted a policy document to committees within the Protocol designed to use market forces to facilitate the transition to non-CFC MDIs, minimize CFC emissions during the transition and provide maximum protection to patients. New CFC-free inhalers have now been developed. A key part of the Consortium's ongoing work will be to retain the exemption in conjunction with coordinating the transition to new products through intensive information and education programmes. Dr Stuart Smith, head of Corporate Communications at 3M UK plc, an IPAC member, highlighted some of the critical success factors influencing the programme:

- spot the issue *early* while the policy situation is still fluid
- ensure that the issue is *actually worth managing*. In this case there were clear business reasons and a moral obligation to the millions of people who rely on their inhalers every day of their lives

- develop a strong case based on *research* and supported by influential *independent endorsers*
- where possible, take your case forward with other companies as a *consortium*, or with other stakeholders as a *coalition* of interest
- ensure that you have access to the right *expertise* when you want it and excellent campaign *coordination and administration*
- remember, in Woody Allen's immortal words, 'the world is run by the people who show up'.

The CFC-inhaler issue is summarized in Figure 4.3.

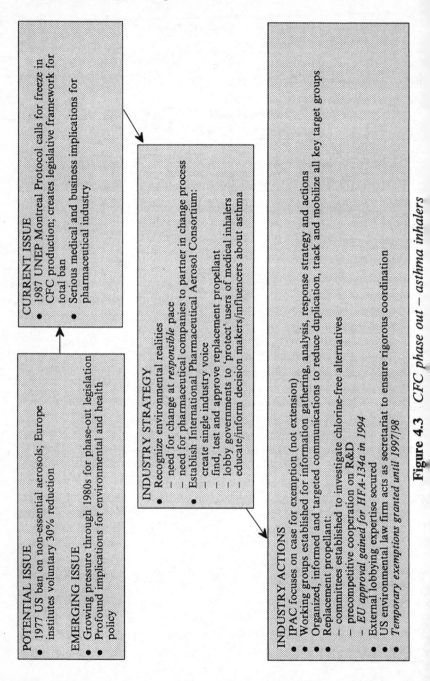

Figure 4.3 *CFC phase out – asthma inhalers*

POTENTIAL ISSUE
● 1977 US ban on non-essential aerosols; Europe institutes voluntary 30% reduction

EMERGING ISSUE
● Growing pressure through 1980s for phase-out legislation
● Profound implications for environmental and health policy

CURRENT ISSUE
● 1987 UNEP Montreal Protocol calls for freeze in CFC production; creates legislative framework for total ban
● Serious medical and business implications for pharmaceutical industry

INDUSTRY STRATEGY
● Recognize environmental realities
  – need for change at *responsible* pace
  – need for pharmaceutical companies to partner in change process
● Establish International Pharmaceutical Aerosol Consortium:
  – create single industry voice
  – find, test and approve replacement propellant
  – lobby governments to 'protect' users of medical inhalers
  – educate/inform decision makers/influencers about asthma

INDUSTRY ACTIONS
● IPAC focuses on case for exemption (not extension)
● Working groups established for information gathering, analysis, response strategy and actions
● Organized, informed and targeted communications to reduce duplication, track and mobilize all key target groups
● Replacement propellant:
  – committees established to investigate chlorine-free alternatives
  – precompetitive cooperation on R&D
  – *EU approval gained for HFA-134a in 1994*
● External lobbying expertise secured
● US environmental law firm acts as secretariat to ensure rigorous coordination
● *Temporary exemptions granted until 1997/98*

5

Implementing an issues management programme

A similar, complementary process to the issues management model described in Chapter 3 can be defined for the role of management decision making at each phase and is shown in Figure 5.1. The *awareness* phase, maps onto the first stage in the issues lifecycle – *potential issue*. Here, the emphasis in the management team is on listening and learning. Those involved need to be alert, open, low-key, inquisitive and challenging. Full use should be made of background information, research and ensuring monitoring infrastructures are in place.

The *exploration* phase indicates an increased urgency over the importance of the issue. Specific responsibilities need to be assigned, organizational awareness is raised and the analysis and opinion formation process begins. Based on working with a number of pharmaceutical companies, an example structure and allocation of responsibilities is shown in Figure 5.2. Typically, in this type of organization, representation should come from medical, safety, regulatory, planning, legal, marketing and communications functions with authority to take specific action. Characteristics of any task force are:

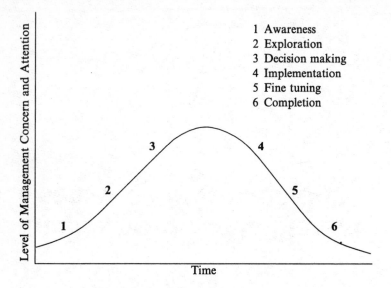

Figure 5.1 *The management process*

- seniority to make decisions, allocate resources and direct programme implementation
- breadth of disciplines represented and appropriate access to information for decision making purposes
- easy access for arranging meetings and 'networking' information; flexibility and informality in working methods
- ability to combine analytical and creative skills with rapid, focused decision making and action
- minimal paper flow to avoid bureaucracy, slow response and leakage of sensitive information.

Broader awareness of the issue in the company is raised at this stage and the analysis and opinion formation process begins.

At the *decision-making* stage the company has to consider action. The management team must objectively assess and decide upon the alternatives presented while still encouraging broad thinking and creativity in the formulation of an action plan.

The *implementation* phase involves taking the necessary steps to make management decisions work in practice, while *fine-*

Roles and Responsibilities:

Task Force
(chair and secretariat)

Communications	Marketing/Sales	Medical	Regulatory	Legal/Planning
• media contact and intelligence gathering	• sales force briefing and training	• review/analysis of data	• liaison with authorities	• impact assessment
• media training	• product education (doctor/patient)	• opinion leader networking	• submission of data	• liability implications
• briefing documentation	• competitive analysis	• study definition/ commissioning	• licence approval status/monitoring	• strategy review
• media briefings/ workshops	• doctor mailings	• data presentation at symposia, medical meetings, workshops, regulatory working groups, etc	• analysis/assessment of approval processes	• counsel
• article drafting and syndication	• medical meetings management			
• crisis communications support	• sales and marketing support materials			

Figure 5.2 *Example task force for a pharmaceutical company*

tuning allows for the measurement and evaluation of current actions and results so that adjustments or enhancements to the action plan can be made.

Completion is the wind-down period which should decrease senior management involvement. Key activities involve appropriate delegation and ensuring implementation of any resulting change management within the organization.

Effective issues management can help to build competitive advantage and sales, particularly in new and emerging markets; it can exploit opportunities or protect corporate policies where there is the potential for major social change. The pressures of market dynamics, competitor activity and resource availability can make it difficult to anticipate, initiate or plan for important issues.

Kerry Tucker and Bill Trumpfheller (1993) have established a five-step plan to help establish an issues management system, which we have found works well in practice.

1. Anticipate issues and establish priorities

This first fundamental step can take many forms, from drawing up a very basic set of assumptions through to a highly elaborate issues anticipation system. Setting up an internal task force, based on the approach outlined in the previous section, is a crucial starting point. Brainstorming sessions and database analysis should focus on responding to questions like:

- What immediate and medium-term competitor, social or regulatory factors do we need to contend with?
- What changes do we anticipate in the marketplace and wider political and social environment over the next 12 months and beyond?
- What factors are likely to affect the way we are working?
- What special events are likely to take place and have an impact on our ability to sustain and develop our markets?

Once these issues are identified, priorities can be set and decisions can be taken on how much time and resource to devote to them.

2. Analyse issues

Develop a formal brief or analysis of the issue, looking at the opportunities and threats against a series of different scenarios. This should cover what could happen if the issue is ignored, and an assessment of how key audiences are likely to be affected by the issue. There should also be a summary of the direction in which the issue is likely to be heading. This will give management a broad view of the issue and its effect on a number of areas such as product market positioning, financial performance, corporate reputation and the potential for regulation or even litigation.

3. Recommend an organizational position on the issue

The analysis from the previous step should provide a database to develop a position designed to create support from the greatest majority of individuals and groups affected. The database is built from answers to the following questions:

- Who is affected?
- How do the affected groups or individuals perceive the issue?
- What are their likely positions and behavioural inclinations?
- What information/data can we gather to support our case?

4. Identify groups and opinion leaders who can advance your position

These groups and individuals should emerge from asking:

- Who makes decisions on the issue?
- Who is likely to support our position?
- Who is likely not to?
- Who can we target successfully to make the biggest difference in advancing our position?

If possible, research should be undertaken to validate assumptions made about groups during the analysis stage. Opinion leaders, closely followed by influential industry or employee associations, consumer and other special interest groups and informed media, can be powerful allies in dealing with a range of audiences, and criteria for selecting them include:

- Who do members of our target groups look to for advice on the issue?
- Who will the (customer, consumer) community and the wider public trust on the issue?
- Who has the credibility to best advance our position on the issue?
- Who is likely to be open to our position on the issue?

5. Identify desired behaviours

This is an easy point to overlook, according to the authors. Advancing specific behaviour relating to the company's position drives development of the rest of the planning processing, namely: communications and marketing strategy, goals, objectives, messages, tactics, resource allocation and budgets.

Finally, evaluation of progress needs to be incorporated into plans to ensure that key milestones are met, the course of the issue is charted, and adjustments made if necessary.

Our experience from dealing with current and historic issues across different industry sectors endorses the value of implementing the following types of activity as early as possible, both to gain the initiative and protect against adverse developments.

Task force set-up

- Identify an appropriately experienced/resourced task force to define and manage issue response strategy.
- Maintain a flexible, creative approach to considering competitive counter-measures, regulatory change and positive corporate positioning initiatives.
- Think positively and proactively throughout – it is easy to be drawn into a defensive strategy from the outset and lose the opportunity to secure or regain the advantage of opinion leader, media and public support.

Intelligence gathering and analysis

- Invest in and establish an early warning intelligence gathering network to monitor, collect and review relevant research/data.
- Constantly assess competitor/regulatory activity and refer to similar, practical experience from other companies for guidance on approach.
- Obtain and monitor relevant peer review/specialist publications as early as possible for assessment and action where appropriate; track trade and broader mass media.

Issue champions

- One way of managing resourcing requirements for information gathering and analysis is for each issue to be assigned to an appropriately experienced individual within the organization. These in-house experts – issue champions – should act as authoritative, up-to-the-minute sources of information to assist task forces and other management in the planning and coordination of related activities.

Background briefing materials

- Prepare background information relevant to desired positioning, eg, key messages, corporate/product/service backgrounders, Q&A, reference contact and research databases, core presentation kits, etc.

Research databases

- In industry sectors where there is the potential for risk to public health, safety or the environment, it is essential to build and maintain technical and scientific databases of information relating to, for example, the long-term safety of a drug, the rigour of hygiene monitoring systems in food processing, the frequency of routine safety checks and actual incident occurrence at manufacturing facilities, the use of independent expert safety audits and impact assessments to encourage best practice techniques for minimizing the risk of chemical or oil spillage, etc.

Relationship management

Build equity *early* through developing and managing influential relationships with:

- supportive academic and other opinion leaders
- informed journalists
- peer review journal editorial boards
- regulatory authorities
- industry and employee associations
- policy units
- political groups at local, national and international levels
- local and other special interest groups.

Do this through informal contact and briefings; information distribution; educational programmes and research sponsorships, etc. These groups communicate informally and formally together, so it is important to understand the linkages between them and the potential for common agendas on issues relating to an organization's positioning. Try to assess their perceptions/opinions on potential issues by classifying them into positive/neutral/negative groupings.

Opinion leader development

- Contact and build relationships with potentially supportive opinion leaders who may become influential, independent endorsers of the company's desired positioning.
- Consider the use of tactics such as research and publication sponsorship, invitations to attend symposia, chair or present data at meetings, round-table discussions where appropriate.

Information/education programmes

- Build support at grass roots level through the organization of community meetings, correspondence, roadshows and provision of training/education aids to encourage more effective understanding and interest. Similar activities should be considered for customer and supplier groups.

Regulatory affairs

- Be prepared to proactively respond to potential regulatory questions relating to organizational, product and service performance.
- Prepare responses and develop relevant information updates that can be regularly mailed to appropriate authorities.
- Organize a meetings programme to build relationships and neutralize potential critical reporting.

Media management

- Work with the media (specialist, general at regional/national and international level as appropriate) proactively by establishing contact, ensuring spokespeople are available, issuing press statements, letters to specialist publications, bylined articles, media briefings and workshops.
- Monitor editorial coverage and individual journalists or publications for interest/bias; classify into positive/neutral/negative editorial stance on an ongoing basis and immediately following major announcements.
- Train appropriate spokespeople – corporate, technical and marketing, and supportive independent opinion leaders where possible.

The 'glocal' approach

- Act local but think global ... in managing issues. Consider implications for other operating companies, the industry as a whole, to decide whether a coalition approach is likely to be more effective, etc.
- Be aware that as the impact of an issue declines in one market, it can easily cross national borders and quickly activate in other countries where local political or competitor agendas may trigger new threats.

Checklists can help

- A checklist to assist in planning an issues management programme is provided below.

Issues Management Checklist

Pre-planning Phase	Responsibility	Timing
1. Audience Identification Identify the key audiences with which you will need to communicate: • academic/other opinion leaders • customers • special interest groups • industry associations • public officials • regulatory authorities • specialist media • national media • international media • other parts of the company • employees • partners/suppliers • competitors. Compile and confirm contact details for all these audiences including the person who normally deals with or contacts them. Establish their relative importance to the issue. Identify their likely perception of and position on the issue (positive/neutral/negative). Determine likely support and availability.		

Pre-planning Phase	Responsibility	Timing
2. Information Requirements Determine the information needs and most appropriate methods of communication for each group. This information includes: • key messages • rationale for position on issue • supporting data and analysis • implications in product and overall commercial strategy context • authorization for the position and agreed process/roll-out of activity involved • communication principles • competitor response analysis • opinion leader and other likely third party 'endorsement'. Identify key messages. Prepare statements, briefing papers and Q&As; seek appropriate approvals. Determine contingency plans and responsibilities for leakage of information to the media; prepare holding statements if necessary. Identify appropriate channels of communication such as presentation of research/data at symposia, workshops and meetings. Identify requirements for presentation materials, briefing packs and invitation letters. Consider formal response requirements for regulatory authorities as appropriate.		

Pre-planning Phase	Responsibility	Timing
Draft letters tailored by audience group, as required. Check with appropriate departments to determine if issue/information distribution is likely to be stock-market sensitive. **3. Method/Process of Communication** Agree a timeline to manage the order and way in which audiences are contacted. Allocate responsibilities for contact process and ensure availability of appropriate 'experts'/managers. Allow for flexibility, particularly in the event of adverse competitor activity. Determine overall media plan – specialist and general – at local, national and international levels as required. (NB: the involvement of national publications and wire services may quickly elevate a perceived issue into one of international importance so anticipation and preparation are essential.) • define complementary contact plan for opinion leaders (and other groups as required) • identify and train company and opinion leader spokespeople; identify single media enquiry point for all incoming telephone calls		

Pre-planning Phase	Responsibility	Timing
• identify publication editorial deadlines for submission of articles/papers. Establish deadlines for participation in relevant conferences/seminars, submission of synopses, booking of facilities, event management planning, etc • allow for adequate preparation and rehearsal time prior to briefings and presentations		

Implementation Phase	Responsibility	Timing
• against pre-agreed action plans, provide updates to inform audiences of the status of the company's position on the issue (external/internal) • consult with key opinion leaders and institutional authorities on a regular basis • monitor media coverage to determine whether balance of commentary is supportive or additional action is required to influence key publications/ broadcast media • set up feedback processes for other audience groups to monitor reactions and determine questions to address in future communications, potential problem areas, etc • consider establishing telephone information lines and cooperation with special interest groups to help answer		

Implementation Phase	Responsibility	Timing
questions or provide educational information as appropriate.		
Allow for flexibility and speed in responding to new situations and in taking the initiative when appropriate. Task force members must be accessible and able to meet at short notice to assess status and agree new actions		
• check progress/fine tune programme elements through regular opinion research and evaluation.		

Summary

While there is never a single generic approach that will work for every issue, this type of framework will help to anticipate, identify and plan a response to potential issues in a methodical and innovative way. Information should always be carefully focused, and briefing papers should have specific objectives that concentrate on realistic outcomes. Defining action in the context of potential bottom-line implications is a good discipline for maintaining this focus.

PART 2

CRISIS MANAGEMENT

6

So it hits the fan – now what?

If you can keep your head when all about you are losing theirs, it's just possible you haven't grasped the situation.

humourist Jean Kerr

In business as in life, crises come in as many varieties as the common cold. The spectrum is so wide it is impossible to list each type. Product-related crises alone range from outright failures as in the case of the widget which resulted in millions of cans of Carlsberg-Tetley bitter being withdrawn from the market in 1995, to unanticipated side effects illustrated by cases of asbestosis and thalidomide. Accidental or deliberate contamination experienced by Lucozade, Perrier and Tylenol and enforced obsolescence as in the case of PCBs are yet two more categories.

However, it is major crises such as airplane and ferry disasters involving tragic loss of life which lead to greatest public interest. It is this type of crisis which leads to the most visible and measurable erosion of public confidence. The public perception of the risk of such events – fuelled by the disproportionate amount of negative publicity – is often out of kilter with the statistical evidence. For example, in the US it would take two 747 crashes per week to equal the number of people killed on US highways in the same period, but automobile crashes rarely make the headlines in the way airplane crashes do.

Advancing technology, which the public has often come to believe to be foolproof, forms yet another category. This category includes the 1967 Apollo spacecraft fire in which three astronauts died, the 1979 'incident' at the Three Mile Island nuclear reactor, the 1986 Challenger space shuttle tragedy, and Chernobyl in April of the same year.

Business crises are often created by mismanagement of the company – injudicious expansion or diversification – evident in cases such as Brent Walker, Next, Saatchi & Saatchi, Blue Arrow/Manpower and Ferranti International. Fraudulent behaviour has led to the demise of some major businesses in recent years of which Barings and BCCI banks are key examples. Increasingly, business crises are the result of the failure to have in place an issues management system which enables companies to spot greater forces at work such as the underlying economic tides of the 1980s boom and the early 1990s recession which billionaire Sir James Goldsmith of Cavenham Foods did and George Walker of Brent Walker didn't.

But the business tribulations of recent years are hardly unique. In 1637, speculation in Dutch tulip bulbs peaked at today's equivalent of more than £500 per bulb and the market collapsed under its own weight, presenting financial nightmares to speculators and their backers.

In 1861, the infant Pony Express in the US met its sudden demise when Western Union inaugurated the first transcontinental telegraph. In 1906, the San Francisco earthquake devastated the city and its banking community – except for A P Giannini, whose small Bank of America continued making loans during the crisis and went on to become one of the world's largest banks – showing that sometimes a crisis can be turned into an opportunity. In 1912 the 'unsinkable' Titanic sank.

William Shakespeare showed a keen business sense when he wrote:

There is a tide in the affairs of men,
Which, taken at the flood, leads on to fortune:
Omitted, all the voyage of their life
Is bound in shallows and in miseries.

Of course, when looking at different corporate crises, hindsight is the best of all management tools. As *Management Today* (1994) has pointed out, a major corporate crisis never fails to provoke – from journalists, investment managers and fellow businessmen – a chorus of exemplary wisdom after the event.

The writing was on the wall months ago, the pundits will claim. You only had to walk down any high street to see it. Surely you could see the board was incompetent, the management deceitful, the auditors complacent, the advisers gutless, the banks irresponsible.

Why didn't 'they' stop George Walker from buying the William Hill chain of betting shops from Grand Metropolitan for £689 million, later pinpointed by Walker himself as the deal that broke the Brent Walker empire? Why didn't the colleagues and advisers who read the draft of Gerald Ratner's 1991 speech to the Institute of Directors, stop him from describing his products as 'total crap'?

The answer is that Walker was overwhelmingly persuasive, that the banks were slavishly keen to back him, that analysts were prepared to argue that a chain of betting shops, with their abundant cashflow, represented a brilliant addition to the Brent Walker portfolio, and that no one at the table had a crystal ball.

In Ratner's case, his upmarket audience thought the joke was funny and true. It was the next day's tabloids, notably the *Sun* which devoted five pages to the story, a story which tore Ratner apart for his mocking insincerity towards the customers who had made him his fortune.

How the mighty fall

No company, no matter how financially successful, powerful or reputable, is immune to crises. Very often, organizations ignore the warning signals which are so obvious in hindsight. Here are three examples in the 'accident' category.

Challenger space shuttle tragedy

In the early 1980s NASA officials, fearful they could not otherwise obtain congressional funding, mounted an energetic public relations campaign which depicted the shuttle as 'all things to all people'. The agency promised the shuttle would lift scientific payloads into orbit, provide the Pentagon with access to the 'high ground' of space, and offer an efficient, economical means of launching communications satellites which would be a highly profitable enterprise. The shuttle's promoters viewed the future through glasses as rosy as those worn by the Soviet engineers who employed nuclear power at Chernobyl to steam-heat the suburbs of Gorky and Odessa.

Faced with spiralling costs and ever-lengthening delays, NASA cut back its training programme, cannibalized parts from other spacecraft and deferred spending half a billion dollars on safety. There was an increasingly wide gap between the facts and the shuttle's glowing public image.

In spite of numerous warnings from NASA engineers – in fact impassioned pleas, unusual for technical people – that the shuttle could not take off in certain temperatures, NASA officials increasingly chose to believe in the image which, in turn, drifted ever further from reality. The odds of a fatal shuttle crash were estimated variously at one in a hundred to one in a hundred thousand. The Challenger mission, the programme's 25th, proved these odds had been incredibly optimistic.

The justification for NASA's trust in its flawed spacecraft was reduced to the fact that it hadn't blown up yet. As at Chernobyl, the accumulation of an impressive safety record in the past came to be taken as a guarantee that nothing could go wrong in the future.

'The argument that the same risk was flown before without failure is often accepted as an argument for the safety of accepting it again', noted Richard Feynman, the Nobel Prize-winning physicist who served on the presidential commission.

But, Feynman added, 'when playing Russian roulette, the fact the first shot got off safely is little comfort for the next'.

It was Feynman who cut through reams of bureaucracy on the O-ring question (which caused the space shuttle failure) by simply immersing a piece of O-ring material in a bucket of iced water during a break in the committee hearings and noting it grew brittle. The trouble with NASA's belief in its own press clippings, Feynman said, was that nature had not read them. 'Reality must take precedence over public relations for nature cannot be fooled' he concluded.

The Challenger disaster set back the NASA programme by decades.

Clapham rail disaster

The official report of the public inquiry into the Clapham rail disaster was a wide-ranging criticism of management and working practices within British Rail. The causes of the accident on 12 December 1988, which claimed the lives of 35 people, injured 500, 69 of them seriously, ranged from the detail of wiring work to mismanagement at a senior level.

The accident happened at 0810 hours. The driver of the 0718 train from Basingstoke to Waterloo stopped his train at signal WF47 just outside Clapham Junction station. He did so in the faith that the signal behind him, WF138, would be at red.

It is a signal's role to act as a sentry. Once a train has passed it onto the section of track it guards, then the signal should turn to red to ensure no other train occupies the same portion of track.

But faulty installation of wiring controlling the crucial WF138 signal meant it did not show red as it was meant to. So the 0614 from Poole, heading in the same direction, did not stop. It ploughed into the Basingstoke train, shunting it across the track into the path of a train travelling in the opposite direction.

The inquiry found that the immediate cause of the accident was wiring which had been incorrectly installed so the signal's fail-safe mechanism was overridden. However, the search for the underlying causes of the accident took the report into British Rail's system of supervision and managerial failure.

In assessing what could be learnt from the disaster, the report concluded British Rail's commitment to the absolute safety of its passengers was not supported in practice. The report stated:

> the appearance was not the reality. The concern for safety was permitted to co-exist with working practices which were positively dangerous. This unhappy co-existence was never detected by management and so the bad practices were never eradicated. Working practices, supervision of staff, poor testing of equipment and poor communication at all levels failed to live up to the concept of safety. They were not safe: they were the opposite.

British Rail has since been broken up and sold off in parts.

Piper Alpha catastrophe

On the night of 6 July 1988 the oil production platform, *Piper Alpha,* operated by Occidental Oil in the UK sector of the North Sea, blew up and was completely destroyed. The disaster killed 167 men, 109 of them dying from smoke inhalation. No system existed to lead the men on the platform to safety. Only 61 survived.

A leak of gas condensate, which later exploded, was caused when a pump was activated while, unknown to the control room, it was under repair. A blank flange fitted to a valve was not leak-tight. The initial explosion caused extensive damage and spread fire through the platform. Gas pipelines leading to other platforms in the area ruptured and intensified the blaze.

Lord Cullen, who led and wrote the report on the disaster, concluded Occidental Oil had not provided adequate training to make its work permit system effective; monitoring of the system was inadequate; communication was poor. Action following a 1987 fatality involving a failure of the work permit system had no lasting effect on practice.

The report said Occidental management should have been more aware of the need for a high standard of incident prevention and fire-fighting. They were too easily satisfied that the work permit system was being operated correctly, relying on the absence of feedback of problems as indicating that all was well.

> The management adopted a superficial attitude to the assessment of the risk of major hazard. They failed to ensure emergency training was being provided as intended. The platform personnel and management were not prepared for a major emergency as they should have been. The safety policies and procedures were in place; the practice was deficient.

Occidental Oil was subsequently acquired by another oil company and has vanished as an entity.

Three brief examples of crises in the 'accident' category but some themes are identifiable: the confusion of image with reality; the belief that because it hasn't happened in the past, it won't happen in the future; the vain hope that because 'the procedures' have been written the accident can't happen and, in each case, a failure to communicate at all levels.

Crises in the 'business' category

In the examples of Brent Walker and Ratner, why, instead of shouting 'stop', have the combined forces of non-executive directors, auditors, public relations advisers, investment analysts and journalists been so often complicit in encouraging chief executives to believe in their own infallibility?

These are circumstances which particularly affected – but not exclusively – the kind of entrepreneurial, share-price-driven companies which came to fame in the 1980s. The crises which affected them have tended to be financial rather than operational.

In some famous cases, outright fraud has either temporarily weakened a company (Guinness and Mirror Group) or destroyed it altogether (Barings Bank); in others, excessive appetite for acquisitions, or exposure to property, has stretched the balance sheet to breaking point. In another 'business' category, clever well-focused businesses such as GPA (in aircraft leasing) and Tiphook (in containers) were suddenly revealed to have misread the downturn in their own highly specialized markets.

The common thread here is that, in almost every case, there is one person in charge, usually the founder of the business, a natural optimist, risk-taker and autocrat, perhaps with no more than two or three long-standing associates whom he really takes into his confidence.

Veteran company doctors have been quoted as saying that if there is one reliable indicator of a company that will eventually run into trouble, it's having a charismatic, high profile chairman. Tiphook's founder-chairman Robert Montague, sun-tanned, Ferrari-driving sponsor of the Conservative winter ball, has been cited as a classic example. But this may be an unduly pessimistic view; Richard Branson (Virgin), Alan Sugar (Amstrad) and Anita Roddick (The Body Shop) clearly buck this trend.

None the less, a past president of the Society of Insolvency Practitioners has said the most common misjudgement made by companies in incipient financial difficulties is that they are not quick enough to change the person at the top.

The one sure way to buy the company time when it's on the edge of trouble is to appoint a new chief executive. So long as he can put up a reasonable business plan the banks will almost always give him six months.

Product-related crises

The contamination scare which prompted the withdrawal of millions of bottles of Lucozade from shops throughout Britain (13 November 1991) is a nightmare of a kind which has come to haunt a growing number of consumer product companies over the past two decades.

In 1990 Perrier was forced to recall every bottle of its popular sparkling water worldwide after some were found to contain traces of benzene.

A few years earlier, Tylenol, a headache pill made by Johnson

& Johnson in the US, was temporarily withdrawn after an extortionist laced capsules with cyanide, killing seven people.

The cost of dealing with such recalls can be huge. Industry experts have estimated that the cost of recalling suspect products from shops costs nine times as much as delivering them in the first place.

This pales into insignificance, however, when compared to the costs of lost production and rebuilding public confidence in products once they have been declared safe. Johnson & Johnson is estimated to have spent more than £50 million to recover from the Tylenol crisis, and Perrier twice as much. However, the manner in which each company managed its product crises was entirely different – as were the consequences.

The Tylenol tale

Never in corporate history has an organization in crisis gained as much public and editorial sympathy as Johnson & Johnson did in the US for its conduct throughout the Tylenol-related poisonings and their aftermath. The day before cyanide-laced Tylenol tablets caused deaths in the Chicago area in September 1982, Tylenol commanded 35 per cent of the US adult over-the-counter analgesic market, accounted for some $450 million of annual sales and contributed over 15 per cent of Johnson & Johnson's overall profits.

At first, just three deaths from cyanide poisoning were associated with the capsules. As the news spread, as many as 250 deaths and illnesses in various parts of the US were suspected of being part of a widespread pattern. Eventually enquiries from the media alone were logged at over 2500.

After testing 8,000,000 tablets, Johnson & Johnson found no more than 75 contaminated tablets, all from one batch. The final death toll was seven, all in the Chicago area, but the alarm had been spread nationwide. Surveys showed later that 94 per cent of consumers were aware Tylenol was associated with the poisonings.

Key to the success of the way in which the Tylenol case was handled lay in the assumption of the 'worst possible scenario'.

Ironically, the closest thing the company had to a crisis plan was its credo that its first concern must be for the public and its customers – a credo which ultimately saved its reputation.

To its credit, Johnson & Johnson lost little time in recalling millions of bottles of its extra-strength Tylenol capsules. The company reportedly spent half a million dollars warning doctors, hospitals and distributors of the possible dangers. At the same time, the *Wall Street Journal* wrote: 'the company chose to take a large loss rather than expose anyone to further risk. The "anti-corporation" movement may have trouble squaring that with the devil theories it purveys'.

The company also resisted the temptation to relaunch the product as soon as it was known to be safe and the lunatic who contaminated the capsules had been arrested. At the time the US government and local authorities in Chicago and elsewhere were pushing for new drug safety laws. Johnson & Johnson saw a marketing opportunity and took it by edging out its competitors in the $1.2 billion analgesic market. It was the first in the industry, after the recall, to respond to the 'national mandate' for tamper-resistant packaging and new regulations imposed by the US Food and Drug Administration.

Johnson & Johnson later went on to relaunch the product and win the Silver Anvil Award of the Public Relations Society of America for its handling of the crisis. Within five months of the disaster, the company had recovered 70 per cent of its one-third share of this huge market. The company had clearly positioned itself as the champion of the consumer, given meaning to the concept of corporate social responsibility, and demonstrated communication expertise hard to equal since.

The plaudits which Johnson & Johnson received leading to, most importantly, market share recovery, stemmed from its decision to anticipate the worst. The company could have restricted the recall to the Chicago area and saved itself millions of dollars. Had it done so, however, its Tylenol sales would almost certainly have suffered more dramatic losses because of poison-tampering hysteria. Their losses would have been far more difficult to recover because of continued uncertainty and loss of public trust. What was happening to Tylenol users in Chicago was receiving coast-to-coast television coverage in America. (If you had been sitting in your New York apartment, had seen the news about Tylenol, and then developed a headache would you have rushed out to the corner drugstore to purchase a bottle of Tylenol? Most unlikely.)

What took the fizz out of Perrier

In complete contrast to Johnson & Johnson, when Perrier found traces of benzene in its water, it dismissed the problem as 'a little affair which, in a few days, will all be forgotten'. Less than 24 hours later Perrier shares were falling like ten green bottles off the wall as more contaminated samples were discovered around the world.

In the US the company decided voluntarily to clear millions of bottles from supermarket shelves. The company in France put this down to American wimpishness rather than a real health scare. To some extent the difference in outlook by the two countries was reflected by their marketing techniques. In the US Perrier advertisements proclaimed 'Perrier is Perfect' while in France advertisements claimed '*Perrier C'est Fou*', ie it is crazy, bubbly and enlivens the spirit.

The company's spokesman in France went on to imply consumers in France were less neurotic than in other countries; they didn't worry about such things. Maybe not, but his remarks were reported in other key markets and the company's apparent lack of concern for its customers caused outrage. Company executives in different countries made conflicting statements and clearly no worldwide strategic recall plan was in place.

Under increasing pressure, four days after the initial discovery of the benzene traces in the US, Perrier decided to withdraw the product worldwide amid proclamations that 'with this action we have saved the image of Perrier all over the world'. By then, however, the damage to the product's reputation had been done. The company had been seen to procrastinate and be inconsistent in its messages about the seriousness of the problem. It was ridiculed by the media (in this country particularly by the now defunct *Today* newspaper).

People drink bottled water partly because they think it is chic and partly because they believe it to be purer than tap water. It is certainly marketed on a 'platform of purity'. Implementing a worldwide recall of a key product is a huge decision to take because of the financial consequences, especially when the reality of the size of the problem is tiny. However, the company which is not seen to take seriously the genuine concerns of its customers, does so at its peril.

Research undertaken across Europe by MORI for design company Henrion, Ludlow & Schmidt in 1995, found Perrier's corporate identity to have been the second most damaged as a result of corporate error. The most damaged was believed to be Shell's after the Brent Spar debacle. Interestingly, the survey was conducted in the same year as the Brent Spar issue but *five years after* the Perrier recall. (see Figure 6.1).

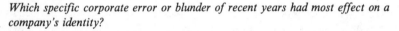
Which specific corporate error or blunder of recent years had most effect on a company's identity?

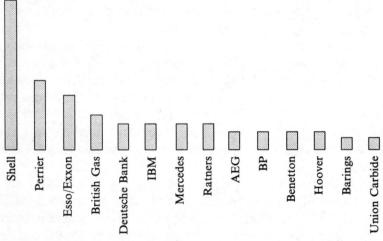

Source: MORI 'Silver Lining 1995'

Figure 6.1 *The effects of crises on different organization's standing*

Even after Perrier's chaotic recall the situation might have been recoverable. A brilliant advertising campaign signalled the end of the problem and that Perrier was back. But it was back, inexplicably, in 750ml bottles instead of the original one litre bottles – yet it cost at least the same amount as the original bigger bottle! The inference seemed to be that customers should pay the cost of the company's own negligence. The company never recovered market share and, with its own share price weakened, became easy prey for a predator. Nestlé soon came along and swallowed it up.

Who will have a crisis?

Next week there can't be any crisis. My schedule is already full.
Dr Henry Kissinger while US Secretary of State

Companies could cite a variety of reasons which prevent them from addressing crisis issues before they occur. Some believe their size, location or the type of business they are in will protect them. Others believe issues and crisis management to be a luxury, or believe crisis is an inevitable cost of doing business. (Indeed, a survey conducted a few years ago among prominent US businessmen found they believed a crisis in business was as inevitable as paying taxes and death.)

In our experience, some executives have difficulty admitting to themselves that their companies could face a crisis because in doing so they would have to question the excellence of their company and, in some cases, even their own professionalism.

Others subscribe to the fallacy that well-managed companies simply do not have crises. This trait can affect even the most public relations conscious companies. Indeed it can affect them more than others. When Nestlé was attacked for selling infant formula in developing countries, where it was often mixed with contaminated water, the company's belief in its own caring, nurturing image made it difficult for senior executives to accept the criticism. There was a prevailing belief that anyone who attacked Nestlé must be a loony or a communist or both.

According to business academic Ian Mitroff, in his book *We're So Big, Nothing Bad Can Happen to Us* (1990), 'how people react to crises provides one of the most powerful windows, if not *the* most powerful window, into the souls of people and their institutions'.

He divides 'crisis-prone' corporations into two types: destructive companies, which believe it is their fundamental right, even their duty, to exploit all human, financial and natural resources for the profit of their shareholders; and tragic companies, which understand the need for change but do not have the emotional or cultural resources to make it happen.

Mitroff cites Exxon Corporation as a 'destructive' company (see Chapter 7) for which little can be done; 'but tragic companies can be helped by outside experts, analysts who can identify problems not apparent to those too close to them and inhibited by fear for their jobs'.

As recently as the early 1990s some companies (especially in the US) even avoided crisis anticipation because of legal liabilities they might assume in doing so. The concern was that if companies identified potential risk areas and failed to guard against them, they might be more responsible legally than if they had not bothered to investigate in the first place.

There used to be an attitude of what you didn't know wouldn't hurt you. Nowadays, however, the courts say if you didn't know you should have known (see Chapter 9).

In this age of corporate accountability, and for all the reasons we have argued in previous chapters, the truth is that no organization is safe from a crisis and the potentially lasting damage it can cause. It is no longer a question of whether a major crisis will strike; it is only a matter of when, which type and how.

What kind of crisis will happen?

In research conducted for us at the start of the 1990s by Business Planning & Research International among senior executives from the *Times Top 1000* companies, the following crises were regarded as most likely to occur:

- environmental pollution
- product defect
- unwanted takeover bid
- sabotage
- death of senior management member
- kidnap of senior management member
- computer breakdown
- industrial dispute
- fraud.

More recent research among senior UK company executives, conducted by Infoplan in 1994, showed a shift in belief as to what kinds of crises might occur. The majority of respondents from 250 major British companies thought sabotage, extortion and product defects were the most likely forms of crises (see Figure 6.2). It is interesting to note the underlying current of optimism here that the most likely forms of crises were seen to be events 'done to the organization', ie, sabotage and extortion, rather than any fault caused by management error – a hope which is certainly at odds with slightly more recent findings from the US.

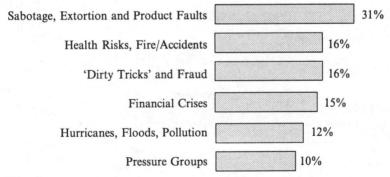

Source: Infoplan International 1994

Figure 6.2 *The most likely causes of crises according to respondents*

Research conducted in 1995 by the Kentucky-based Institute for Crisis Management showed that company executives and consultants had been focusing on the wrong kinds of crises. Business crisis stereotypes such as fires and explosions accounted for only 17 per cent of 1995 crisis news stories. The real problems had revolved around white-collar crime, labour disputes and company mismanagement.

The fastest growing categories in the US were class action lawsuits, executive dismissals, hostile takeovers and sexual harassment – all of which had more than doubled since 1990. The news stories on these management crises were small in number compared to white-collar crime, labour disputes and mismanagement but they invariably attracted the media's attention because of the gut-wrenching personal and professional problems which they surfaced (see Figure 6.3).

This same research also revealed executives not employees had been responsible for most crisis news coverage in the 1990s – management decisions were directly or indirectly involved in 78 per cent of 56,000 crisis news stories.

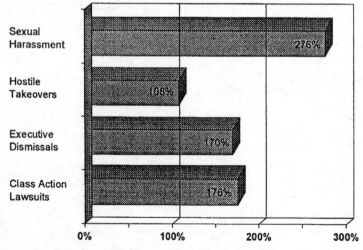

Source: Institute for Crisis Management, Kentucky, USA

Figure 6.3 *Most rapid business crises category growth in the 1990s*

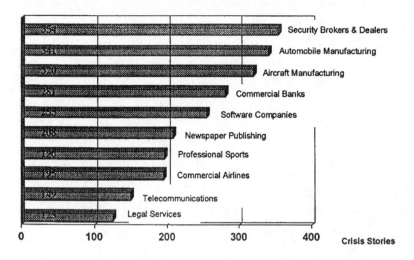

Source: Institute for Crisis Management, Kentucky, USA

Figure 6.4 *Most crisis prone industries in 1995*

The most crisis-prone US industries in 1995, measured by the number of crisis news stories devoted to them, are shown in Figure 6.4.

For the purposes of the remainder of this book we are going to use our own definition of a crisis:

> an event which causes the company to become the subject of widespread, potentially unfavourable, attention from the international and national media and other groups such as customers, shareholders, employees and their families, politicians, trade unionists and environmental pressure groups who, for one reason or another, have a vested interest in the activities of the organization.

Summary

- Beware the obsequiousness of advisers.
- Don't confuse image with reality.
- Don't believe it can't happen because it hasn't before.
- Don't believe that writing the 'procedures' will prevent it from happening.
- Communicate at all times at all levels.
- Faced with disaster, consider the worst possible scenario.
- Be prepared to demonstrate human concern for what has happened.
- Never underestimate genuine concerns of customers.

7

Perception *is* the reality

Are you going to believe what you see or what I'm telling you?
Groucho Marx

Virtually every crisis contains within itself the seeds of success as well as the roots of failure. Finding, cultivating and harvesting the potential success is the essence of crisis management. The essence of crisis *mis*management is to make a bad situation worse. Many would argue, for example, that President Nixon's cover-up of the Watergate break-in created a bigger crisis than the original transgression would have produced.

Successful management of a crisis situation is about recognizing you have one, taking the appropriate actions to remedy the situation, being *seen* to take them and being *heard* to say the right things. Companies often misclassify a problem, focusing on the technical aspects and ignoring issues of perception – as we have seen with Intel's Pentium chip and Shell's response to Greenpeace over the disposal of the Brent Spar.

When Intel finally offered to replace the defective chip only an estimated 1 to 3 per cent of individual consumers (who constitute two-thirds of the purchasers of computers with

Pentium chips) took up the offer. It wasn't that people wanted a new chip; it was just that they wanted to know they could get a new chip if they wanted one. As everyone knows, banks don't want borrowers to pay off their loans; they just want to know that borrowers *can* pay off their loans.

The problem in this stage of crisis management is that perception truly does become reality. In the case of Shell and Brent Spar, as the *Wall Street Journal* reported at the time: 'Shell made a strategic error. In a world of sound bites one image was left with many viewers: a huge multinational oil company was mustering all its might to bully what was portrayed as a brave but determined band'. Whatever the reality of the situation, Shell found itself floundering on the shoals of worldwide media perception.

Ordinary people couldn't get their heads round Shell's scientific and environmental arguments. The company's response focused almost entirely on the print media when television is by far more the most influential, and therefore important, medium. The television pictures showed water cannons being sprayed at the 'brave but determined band'.

Exxon Corporation's handling of the Valdez oil spill also taught students of crisis management important lessons in how poor communication can create a perception which does not reflect the reality – lessons we observed and did our best to remember when we were called in to help with the Braer disaster off the Shetland Islands in 1993 and the Sea Empress disaster in Milford Haven, Wales, in 1996.

A tale of three sorry tankers

Exxon Valdez: how pouring oil on water created plenty of troubles

On 24 March, 1989, at 2100 hours, the 987-foot Exxon Valdez oil tanker left the harbour of South Alaska's Valdez and entered Prince William Sound bound for California. The seas were calm and the weather was good. A local pilot, who had guided the super-tanker out of the port, was taken off shortly after 2330 hours. Twenty minutes later the *Exxon Valdez* ploughed into rocks and America's worst oil spill disaster had begun. Ten million gallons of oil spewed out of the vessel into Prince William Sound, a rich natural habitat. The disaster became instant world news.

Exxon, one of the five largest companies in the United States, had been under the leadership of Lawrence G Rawl since 1986. The son of a truck driver, an ex-marine, and with 37 years as an employee of Exxon before becoming chairman, Rawl was known for having a strong dislike of publicity and journalists. He perceived the media as a danger, to be avoided at all costs.

When the media asked for a comment at Exxon's headquarters in Houston several hours after the disaster it was told this was a matter for the Exxon Shipping Company. They could not and did not want to make any further comment. When asked if the chairman would be interviewed on television, the response was that the chairman of the board had no time for that kind of thing.

Later, a spokesperson for Exxon Shipping coolly informed the press that emergency procedures and manuals existed for such events. Meanwhile the entire world was watching televised pictures of these emergency procedures failing as thousands of birds, otters and seals died in the oil slick.

Emergency procedures should apparently have been initiated by the Alyeska Pipeline Company, a consortium of seven oil companies who use the Alaskan pipeline. In the event of disaster, the consortium would be the first to act. But in this case even the most basic steps were not taken, and a ship specially designated for fighting oil pollution was left sitting in the dock for some time.

After more than a week Exxon was still pursuing a policy of 'no comment'. The publicity became so hostile that eventually Frank Iarossi, the director of Exxon Shipping, flew to Valdez to hold a press conference. This ended in a bitter battle with fishermen and journalists. Iarossi retaliated and the one small opportunity to cooperate and communicate with the press was lost. Iarossi's subsequent daily briefings were likened to the press conferences during the Vietnam War: generals who summed up small successes only to be immediately confronted by journalists who had seen completely different things on the battlefields.

Suddenly the chairman, Lawrence Rawl, decided to appear on television. He was interviewed 'live' and watched by millions of extremely angry Americans right across the US. The first question put to him concerned the latest plan for the clean-up. He hadn't read it. He explained: 'it is not the role of the chairman of a large worldwide corporation to read every technical plan'. His arrogance was blatant.

When asked about the public relations disaster his company was facing – Esso products were being boycotted in the US by this time – he replied: 'the reason we've got this public relations disaster (admitting he had one) is because of the media's reporting of the situation'. He proceeded to place the blame for his company's problems at the feet of the world's press. He showed no emotion over the enormous environmental disaster and offered no apologies to fishermen whose livelihood had been destroyed.

He didn't bother to go to Alaska to see for himself the damage which had been done until a fortnight after the event. When he did go the media was kept unaware of his visit. The damage to Exxon's reputation was complete.

The consequences for the company and the rest of the industry were dire. It is estimated the spill cost the company – in fines, clean-up expenses and lost market share – at least $7 billion. The company slipped from being the largest oil company in the world to the third largest.

New legislation was imposed on the oil tanker industry requiring all new ocean-going tankers to be built with double hulls. Experts in the shipping industry suggest double hulls are potentially more dangerous than single hulls because of the risk of a build-up of gas between the two hulls. Having seen the Braer and Sea Empress disasters first hand, it is easy to form the view that four hulls would not have prevented those oil spills.

The new legislation appears to be a cosmetic, knee-jerk political reaction by governments who felt they had to be seen to 'police' the wicked oil tanker and oil industries – a perception of wickedness created by Exxon's appalling communication in the aftermath of the Valdez spill.

Lessons from Exxon Valdez

When a tanker spills millions of gallons of oil into the sea, or an aeroplane falls out of the sky, or a ferry turns turtle in Zeebrugge harbour, people's first reaction is one of shock. It is difficult to accept that such disasters can still occur in this age of advancing technology and environmental-consciousness. But, ultimately, no one expects there to be a zero-risk associated with any industry. Accidents do happen whether in our private lives or in business.

This initial sense of shock, however, quickly turns to anger if the company at the centre of the crisis is not seen to take the appropriate action and to say the appropriate words. People need to be quickly reassured about certain things, essentially that:

- everything (hopefully) was in place to try and prevent the accident from happening in the first place
- none the less, given the nature of the industry the company works in, it had the foresight to anticipate the possibility of such an event occurring and knew what to do to remedy the situation as far as possible, and as quickly as possible. In other words, to have the ability to paint a picture in words of a group of competent, caring people who swung into action really quickly to handle the situation
- *the company really cares about what has happened.*

Exxon failed miserably on all three counts. In the aftermath of disaster, no action demonstrates more a company's concern for what has happened than the top man or woman being seen to go to the site, to be seen to take personal charge of the aftermath, and to communicate three simple messages:

- This is what has happened.
- This is what we are doing about it.

- This is how we feel about what has happened.

People will still feel aggrieved by what has happened but the anger will be dissipated if the company is seen to do its best in what is likely to be the most difficult of all circumstances. It is people's anger which causes the lasting damage to organizations. It leads to product boycotts, shares being sold and more demanding restrictions and penalties.

Braer: behind the headlines

During the course of 5 January 1993, we watched on the office television the events following the Braer oil tanker's grounding on rocks off the Shetland Islands earlier that day. At 5pm we received a telephone call from New York. It was the chairman of Ultramar Inc. whose oil formed the cargo of the Braer. Could we help?

He told us he was catching the overnight flight to Heathrow and would then fly to Aberdeen where we were to rendezvous the following morning. Michael Regester takes up the story.

I booked myself on the last flight that evening from Heathrow to Aberdeen. The plane was packed with journalists and press photographers all headed for the same destination.

From Aberdeen I called the oil journalist Philip Algar, already on the Islands. Philip had travelled to the Shetlands, not in his capacity as a journalist but in response to a request from the owners of the Braer to act as their media adviser. He brought me up-to-date with the facts.

The 89,000 dwt tanker, carrying 84,000 tonnes of crude oil from Norway to Quebec, lost engine power early in the morning of 5 January. The owners believe pipes probably damaged an air vent, resulting in sea-water entering the fuel tanks.

The vessel subsequently went aground at Garth's Ness on Shetland. Dreadful weather, with winds up to 100 mph, thwarted salvage attempts. By the end of the week the entire cargo was spilled, causing considerable loss of wildlife and inflicting immediate damage on a part of the local salmon fishing industry.

Ironically, the bad weather responsible for the accident played a major role in dispersing the oil rapidly. Within a few weeks, the tourist authority stated: 'everything for the summer visitor season is now back to normal. Indeed, if you missed the news of the Braer, and now visited Shetland, there is nothing whatsoever to indicate that the islands came close to such a disaster'.

The trouble was, you would have to have been a Martian to have missed the news of the Braer. Within 48 hours of the accident there were over 500 journalists on the Islands, all based at the tiny Sumburgh airport at the southern end of Shetland. The scenes were amazing. Shetland is not renowned for its over-capacity of hotels or cars for hire. Journalists were knocking on people's doors, asking: 'How much for a room for a few nights and the use of your car?' The nearest hotel we could obtain rooms at was 60 miles away. The two showers at Sumburgh airport had been rented out as editing suites to the BBC and ITN.

I had booked a private room at Aberdeen airport to brief the Ultramar chairman on the latest situation and organized a charter plane to take us on to the Shetlands after his arrival. All commercial flights were booked up for days.

When we are called into crisis situations, often at a moment's notice, it is usually by companies for which we have never worked before. The situation is already highly pressurized by the time we get there and it is important to establish a quick and trusting rapport with the senior people we are dealing with. As I shook hands with the Ultramar chairman and was about to bring him up-to-date our flight was called. Our takeoff slot had been brought forward.

Once onboard it was impossible to have a conversation such was the noise from the tiny plane bouncing around in 100 mph winds. Knowing we were likely to be surrounded by the media on arrival at Sumburgh I gave the chairman a copy of the statement I had hoped to discuss with him in Aberdeen. I waited with some anxiety as he read it for this was to be a critical moment in the establishment of our relationship.

One of our golden rules concerns the order in which statements are made in crisis situations. Whether written or spoken they must always cover the following topics in the following order:

- people
- environment
- property
- money.

This is simply because this is the order in which most newspapers and broadcast media will cover the story. But sometimes our clients, not unusually on the advice of lawyers, don't agree and prefer to say something banal like: 'We will issue a statement when we have all the facts'. I need not have worried. The chairman agreed with the statement and proved to be an excellent communicator.

Press conferences were held twice a day for the next few days. When dealing with such large numbers of journalists and television crews this is the only practical way of keeping them up-to-date (see Chapter 11). Philip Algar and I were keen for our respective clients to be represented at the press conferences organized by the Shetland Islands, in order to present a united team dealing with the situation. This was agreed.

At the first press conference in which we participated, Ultramar's chairman had only about five per cent of press questions directed at him. The vast majority were aimed at the owners of the Braer and the Shetland Islands Council which was in charge of the clean-up. I therefore suggested we participate in no more press conferences but advised the chairman to remain on the Islands in case ownership of the crude oil became an issue. He should not be seen to be 'running away' from the situation but I didn't want him as a sitting target if there was no interest in the oil's ownership.

Instead, we focused on giving one-to-one interviews for the North American press who had arrived and in assessing for ourselves the amount of damage to the Islands. In crises of this kind it is important to obtain your own record of what has happened – particularly for dealing with future insurance claims and assisting with official investigations (see Chapter 9).

I hired a filmcrew from Aberdeen. They wanted to fly over but we asked them to take the ferry so they could bring a car with them. That solved our own transport problem as well as providing us with the footage we needed. Later, the footage had an additional use when it was turned into a film for Ultramar employees and investors back in the States.

In crisis situations a primary consideration must, of course, be audiences. Who needs to know what and how quickly? While messages to each audience must be consistent it is not always possible to transmit them all at the same time to each audience. In the case of the Braer the key immediate audience for Ultramar was its shareholders. After all, everyone in the financial community knew the Valdez spill had cost Exxon $7 billion. Ultramar was a tiny organization in comparison. If its shareholders thought they were going to be facing a bill of similar proportions, what was going to happen to the share price? So a first action taken by the company was to get its shares suspended on the New York Stock Exchange until it could assess the company's likely amount of financial liability, and check it had the insurance policies in place to meet the liability. Having done this the situation was explained to shareholders and their advisers and, later that day, trading in the shares was resumed. In the event, they dropped just 25 cents on the previous day's price.

The 'information void'

> The vacuum caused by a failure to communicate is soon filled with rumour, misrepresentation, drivel and poison.
> Business academic C Northcote Parkinson

Meanwhile the appalling weather conditions on the Islands were preventing workers from stemming the leaking oil and helicopters from spraying dispersant. In fact, nothing was happening. This absence of activity led to an 'information void' – typical in a crisis situation.

Instead of communicating positive messages about what

would be done to minimize the environmental damage once the weather had subsided, virtually nothing was communicated by those responsible for the clean-up.

The void was instantly filled with media reports that the Islands were 'covered with oil', that 'oil was carcinogenic' – you could get leukemia from breathing the fumes. As a consequence, 'school children were being evacuated', 'sheep were being evacuated' and 'all the salmon fish farms were contaminated'. And so the media pollution went on.

After oil, the two most important industries in the Shetland Islands are the export of salmon to Japan, and tourism. Following the media reports, the Japanese refused to import any more salmon and tourism fell right away. In that year alone, the Shetland Islands Council reported a £1.3 million loss in tourism revenues and forecast a cumulative loss of £18.2 million by 1998. The public perception of the situation had become the reality.

These lessons were uppermost in our minds when we were called in by the Wales Tourist Board on 15 February 1996, after the Sea Empress hit rocks on its approach to Texaco's refinery in Milford Haven.

Sea Empress in distress

The Wales Tourist Board had a huge challenge on its hands to prevent a similar impact on Welsh tourism. Tourism in Wales generates about £1.4 billion per year and is directly responsible for employment of one in nine of the workforce.

The protracted delay in the salvage operation only fuelled the daily saturation coverage of oiled beaches and birds. Media reports in Germany, Denmark and further afield implied the whole of Wales was affected. The task in hand was to correct these misconceptions and convert the massive exposure of Pembrokeshire in the world media into an advantage.

Our strategy, which won immediate approval from the Wales Tourist Board, had to be aimed at supporting the tourist trade, reassuring holiday-makers and persuading the media that every possible effort was being made to clean the affected beaches and restore them to their natural state prior to the tourist season.

Less than a week after the spill the Welsh Tourism Fights Back campaign was underway. Colleague Rosie Clifford devised the theme: 'The Treasure is Still Here – But No Longer a Secret'. This was a reference to the Pembrokeshire coastline being known as the 'secret treasure of Wales'. The theme struck a chord and the 'treasure' frequently appeared in newspaper headlines.

We wanted to minimize the medium- and long-term damage to the tourist industry by capitalizing on the rapid and comprehensive clean-up operation; and to emphasize that only a small area of Wales had suffered. The majority of Pembrokeshire's beaches were unaffected. This would hopefully counteract the predominantly negative and exaggerated image of the extent of environmental pollution propagated by media coverage.

The campaign included:

- a telephone hotline to respond to holiday-makers concerned about their bookings; and to monitor public concern
- organizing over 20 television and radio interviews for the Wales Tourist Board's chief executive, John French – over a critical 48-hour period when the issue was still headline news – to convey agreed messages
- transmitting positive messages to key UK and overseas markets via British tourism offices overseas
- consulting with Texaco, owners of the crude oil cargo, tourist operators, accommodation and attraction owners, local authorities and other agencies to ensure consistent messages to key audiences
- briefing HRH Prince of Wales and the Secretary of State for Wales on the campaign to gain their support.

The words of Wales Tourist Board chief executive John French summed up the passion and rigour with which the potentially damaging information void was filled to best advantage: 'the images which brought us worldwide attention were negative but now more people than ever before know of the beauty that can be found here. We were determined not to let the media's images outlast the pollution itself'.

Positive media coverage immediately began to outweigh the

negative. On one day alone – St David's Day – the Wales Tourist Board press office broadcast its reassurance campaign live through 25 local radio stations reaching in excess of an estimated 1,000,000 listeners throughout the UK.

A study jointly published in July 1996 by the Welsh Economy Research Unit, University of Wales, Cardiff Business School and the Welsh Institute of Rural Studies, entitled *The Economic Consequences of the Sea Empress Spillage* (1996) concluded:

> the weighted anticipated impact of the spillage on tourism spending in Pembrokeshire in 1996 was an average reduction of 12.9 per cent and slightly less for south west Wales overall. Applying this average impact, supported by actual turnover experience in the early parts of 1996, to the total estimated tourism spend in Pembrokeshire in 1995 of £160 million, gives a gross estimated impact on tourism spending in Pembrokeshire of £160m × −12.9% = £20.64 million.

From a potential total loss of revenue from tourism expenditure in Pembrokeshire, and severe reduction in expenditure in other parts of Wales, the damage had been limited to 12.9 per cent. For once, the perception had more or less matched the reality.

Summary

- Recognize you have a crisis.
- Be seen to take the appropriate actions.
- Be heard to say the right things.
- Remember television is the most important medium.
- Don't blame the media for your problems; it can be your best friend.
- People's anger leads to product boycotts, fall in share price and more demanding restrictions and penalties.
- Talk about people first, then the environment and property and, finally, money.
- Don't be a sitting target at press conferences.
- Anticipate the 'information void' and be prepared to fill it.
- Remember 'media pollution' can outlast environmental pollution and be more damaging economically.

8

The media in crisis situations

Four hostile newspapers are more feared than a thousand bayonets.

Napoleon Bonaparte

The chairman of Exxon's fear and distrust of the media became a self-fulfilling prophecy for him. Ignoring the media when dealing with issues and crises will always prove to be a catastrophic error of judgement. This may seem obvious but it is a mistake often made by organizations facing a tricky, potentially disastrous, situation.

For example, in the immediate aftermath of the Lockerbie disaster, Pan Am made a conscious decision to minimize communication with the press. The airline believed a policy of non-communication would somehow distance Pan Am's name from the tragic consequences of the disaster.

This was a huge error of judgement. In a situation like this the media will descend on the site of the accident like a plague of locusts which needs to be fed. If it isn't fed by the organization which finds itself, however inadvertently, at the centre of the crisis, it will feed from the hands of others. And become deeply suspicious of the hand which obviously isn't feeding it.

When questioned about the warning of a possible terrorist attack, Pan Am initially said it was unaware of any warning. It was later revealed that all carriers operating in Europe, including Pan Am, had been informed. A cardinal public relations principle had been breached. Concealing the truth is simply not an option. There are too many eager sources and too many eager reporters. In crisis situations, it is imperative *to tell your own story, to tell it all and to tell it fast.*

So did Pan Am's CEO, Thomas Plaskett, go to Lockerbie, apologize, attend memorial services, atone for responsibility? He did not. The media made mincemeat of the airline. It was already in financial difficulty and the trans-Atlantic route was its only remaining profitable one. Passengers lost confidence in the airline – in its willingness and ability to transport us safely from one side of the Atlantic to the other – and chose other airlines in preference. The boycott proved to be the final nail in the airline's financial coffin. It went bankrupt.

How JAL and British Midland got it right

In contrast, when JAL suffered its worst-ever crash on 12 August 1985 – 520 people died – the airline followed an elaborate protocol to atone. Personal apologies were made by the company's president, memorial services were held and financial reparations paid. For weeks, more than 400 airline employees helped bereaved relatives with everything from arranging funeral services to filling in insurance forms. All advertising was suspended voluntarily. Had JAL not made these acts of conciliation, it would have courted charges of inhumanity and irresponsibility.

At the memorial service, JAL's president, Yasumoto Takagi, bowed low and long to relatives of the victims, and to a plaque bearing the victim's names. He asked forgiveness, accepted responsibility and offered to resign. The maintenance chief committed suicide.

Marion Kinsdorf, a US business academic, has pointed out in

Public Relations Review (1990):

> the airline's reaction reveals not only the Japanese tendency towards 'group think' but the consciousness of equality of each member of the group. In Japan, what is regarded as 'just' or 'moral' is what everyone in a particular group, at a particular place and time, thinks is right. As a result, the spokesperson or the president of an airline responds and behaves according to how the majority defines 'just and proper'. Hence, news is received differently.
>
> JAL's president's visibility, his offer to resign, becomes more symbolic. He was responding to deep thoughts and feelings. In a country where nonverbal communication is far more crucial and effective than the spoken, such an act of resignation becomes a nonverbal expression of apology.

From the day of the accident, JAL had mobilized its staff, from the president down, to offer gestures of apology and regret. When family members had to travel to a small mountain village to identify bodies, airline staff accompanied them, paying all expenses, bringing them food and drink and clean clothes. It spent $1.5 million on two elaborate memorial services and dispatched executives to every victim's funeral (although some were asked to leave). It also established a scholarship fund for children whose parents died in the crash.

Importantly also, JAL were quick to notify victims' families. Overnight it issued lists of passenger names. One relative of a victim on Pan Am's flight 103 was not told officially of her husband's death until six weeks after the crash.

Although JAL did suffer from some media criticism, and for a while lost market share, it eventually made a full recovery. Much of its response was driven by Japanese culture. One would not, after all, expect the chief maintenance engineer of a western airline to commit suicide. But its response was seen, crucially by the media, to be humane, caring and responsible.

A similar response came from British Midland Airways when one of its Boeing 737s crashed near Kegworth alongside the M1 motorway just a few weeks after the Lockerbie crash.

The airline's chairman, Sir Michael Bishop, immediately

raced to the scene of the accident giving live radio interviews from his car phone. His voice was patched in to a live interview with Michael Buerk on the BBC's *Nine O'Clock News*.

His response was remarkable. Many people in senior managerial positions, fearful of being misreported by the media – and of the consequences of being misreported – won't give media interviews until they have all of the facts at their fingertips and have worked out all the answers to the potentially most difficult questions. In a crisis situation this can be disastrous not least because it will usually take many hours before this is possible. Communication *has* to begin immediately.

Sir Michael Bishop gave interviews when he had no knowledge about the cause of the accident; how many people had died, been injured, or had survived. Lack of information at the outset of a crisis is typical. Very little information will be available for several hours. Some facts will be known – 'one of our planes has crashed' – but not much else.

Faced with this dilemma, Sir Michael Bishop focused on expressing how he felt about what had happened and what he was going to do about the situation. He immediately began to 'manage' the flow and content of news to the media.

In essence, he said he was going to do everything in his power to ensure the families of victims were looked after properly, the injured received the best possible treatment; and no stone would be left unturned in establishing the cause of the accident to try and prevent such an accident from happening again.

There was not much 'content' to what he said but he understood and implemented one of the golden rules of crisis communication – begin it at once, from the top of the organization. Even though it was eventually found to have been pilot error which caused the crash, no one lost confidence in British Midland or in Boeing 737s. Ironically, some people have argued the airline's reputation was actually enhanced by the chairman's response. It was seen to be caring and responsible.

Gaining media support

This may come as a surprise, but in our experience of dealing with the media in crisis situations its attitude will be, to begin with, at worst neutral and at best sympathetic – particularly if people have died or been injured. It is usually when the media believe the organization at the centre of the crisis is unduly slow in providing information, reticent about providing 'talking heads' for interview or thought to be withholding information, that it becomes hostile. The key to successful communication in crisis situations is to establish the organization at the centre of the crisis as *the single authoritative source of information about what has happened and what is being done about it.*

International research has shown the media to be by far the most credible source of information throughout the western world, well ahead of governments and, with the possible exception of Italy, the church. By virtue of its 'believability' the media acts as the most important conduit to shaping people's beliefs and behaviour.

Ultimately, newspapers, television and radio news programmes are 'products'. Those which best meet the demands of the prevailing market sell the most or are watched and listened to the most. Those that don't get it right either go out of business (the *Today* and *Sunday Correspondent* newspapers are examples) or suffer a drop in sales or audiences.

The *Sun*, for example, suffered a drop in sales when it attacked pop singer Elton John. It underestimated the singer's popularity with its readers and the libel cost it £1 million in compensation. Similarly, the newspaper's sales dropped after its reporting of the Hillsborough tragedy.

Hillsborough: how the media can have its own crises

Newspaper comment is free but facts are sacred.
                              newspaper editor in 1926, C P Scott

Few tragedies have been so comprehensively recorded as the disaster at the FA Cup semi-final between Nottingham Forest and Liverpool at Sheffield's Hillsborough stadium in April 1989. As Lord Justice Taylor's enquiry was later to state, the deaths of 95 Liverpool fans had been a wholly avoidable tragedy, but one which had been long in the making.

Peter Chippindale and Chris Horrie provide a remarkable insight into the *Sun's* handling of the Hillsborough tragedy in their book *Stick It Up Your Punter – the rise and fall of the Sun* (1992). They point out how Taylor's acerbic report threw into sharp relief the way the football authorities had connived with papers like the *Sun* to hype the former working-class game into the realms of television-led fantasy. Multi-million pound transfer fees for players had soaked up the money desperately needed to update ancient grounds and squeezed smaller clubs to the extent that facilities had deteriorated into shabby squalor. Taylor summed it up as 'the all-pervading stench of fried onions' and the sight of 'men urinating against walls because of the inadequate and foul toilet facilities' (Lord Justice Taylor, 1990).

The Hillsborough tragedy, as Taylor bluntly concluded, was primarily the fault of the South Yorkshire police in charge of crowd control. To relieve the increasingly lethal pressure of 5000 Liverpool fans struggling to get through the bottleneck of the turnstiles, the police had given the order for the gates to be thrown open. But instead of routing the surging fans on to empty terraces, they had allowed them to take the route through a tunnel into one of the pens which was already overcrowded. From here there was no escape because of the wire cages enclosing the front.

As the inevitable push forward began, Superintendent David Duckenfield, in charge of the police, 'froze' in his control box and made matters worse by treating the fans' desperate attempts to escape by scaling the cage as a 'pitch invasion'. Only when it was too late did he allow the emergency gates to be opened, relieving the pressure.

Every second of the drawn-out horror unravelled itself, live, in front of a television audience expecting an exciting afternoon's viewing. The mass of sports photographers took thousands of pictures, many of which showed such harrowing detail of death and suffering it was almost impossible to decide which could be printed. Some people would bay for the blood of the papers printing the most horrific pictures while others would pile into the shops to buy the ones with the most shocking images.

Deciding what words could be written about the tragedy should have been easier. However, the then editor of the *Sun*, Kelvin MacKenzie, chose words which turned the Hillsborough tragedy into an unparalleled journalistic disaster, with huge financial consequences.

On the Monday after the accident the *Sun* cleared page after page for different pictures and stories, pulled together under the tacky headline: 'Gates of Hell'. On the Sunday immediately after the match, newspapers had sold an extra 500,000 copies between them. On the Monday, public desire for more detail still seemed insatiable.

The *Sun*, like other dailies, had more time to reflect on which pictures to use. But as the official death list had not been published there was still no way it could tell in most cases whether the individuals pictured being crushed or lying on the pitch were now alive or dead. Like most of its rivals, it printed them regardless of causing unbelievable anguish to families and friends of victims.

It was not the *Sun* but the *Daily Mirror* with its use of colour, so making the pictures even more ghoulish, which brought the wrath of Liverpool down on its head on Monday morning. The editor's justification was that showing the full horror of the event would help to ensure nothing like it could happen ever again. One wonders if he would have used the same pictures had they depicted one of his own children?

During the Monday a new and more sinister factor began to surface in the story. From the start there had been an understandable knee-jerk reaction of blaming hooligans for the disaster, and it was this preconditioning which had largely accounted for Superintendent Duckenfield's automatic assumption of a pitch invasion. Even when most of the deaths had already occurred, television commentators had fallen into the same trap by excitedly screaming that fans were tearing down the hoardings. They were – but only to use as makeshift stretchers.

On the Tuesday morning the *Sun* started to blame hooliganism for the tragedy. It asked: 'Is it fair to make the police the scapegoat for the disaster? It happened because thousands of fans, many without tickets, tried to get into the ground just before kick-off – either by forcing their way in or by blackmailing the police into opening the gates'.

The next day it went the whole hog. Beneath a huge headline, 'THE TRUTH' it stated:

- Some fans picked pockets of victims.
- Some fans urinated on the brave cops.
- Some fans beat up a PC giving the kiss of life.

The story began: 'Drunken Liverpool fans viciously attacked rescue workers as they tried to revive victims of the Hillsborough soccer disaster, it was revealed last night'. A 'high-ranking' police officer was quoted as saying: 'The fans just acted like animals. My men faced a double hell – the disaster and the fury of the fans who attacked us'.

This was an outrageous libel of all the people involved but was legally safe because no names were used – as Liverpool City Council found out later when it debated suing the paper. The people of Liverpool did the only thing they could do. They turned their anger on the newspaper itself.

Some newsagents put it under the counter; some refused to sell it. Granada TV news showed people burning copies. All over the city copies of the paper were being ripped up, trampled and spat upon. People carrying it in the street found it snatched out of their hands and torn to shreds in front of them; the paper disappeared entirely from Ford's plant at Halewood and dozens of landlords banned it from their premises. Sales of the newspaper in Liverpool collapsed.

Newsagents slashed their orders by as much as 80 per cent.

The *Mirror*, which had raised £1 million for the disaster fund by increasing its cover price, was piling into Liverpool to seize the opportunity it had been given and rapidly gained ground despite its original ghoulish pictures.

The newspaper industry had learnt that, like any other industry, people won't buy products which have been 'contaminated'. Sales of the paper on Merseyside have never recovered to former levels.

The media as an ally

In most cases, the media will act responsibly if it is handled in an open and honest way. Public relations activity in crises must never attempt to hide the facts of what has happened; it has to act as a facilitator to explain what has happened and as a 'driver' to ensure appropriate action is seen to be taken to remedy, as far as possible, what has gone wrong. To deliberately hide the facts is complete folly. Sooner or later, they will be discovered and the situation will become worse because of accusations of a 'cover-up'.

There will always be some who view crisis management as a 'black art' and will not believe anything said to them. In our experience they are in the minority. There are some television programmes where the company will always be on a hiding-to-nothing because of their anti-business bias: *Panorama* and *Watchdog* are examples.

For example, on one edition of *Watchdog* in 1996 the programme had, in its view, cunningly placed hidden cameras and some valuables in cars to see if they would be stolen by employees of car valeting companies. Probably to its surprise, at some valeting premises the valuables were not stolen but returned to their owner. The programme did not bother to mention the names of those companies but of course told us the names of those which had pocketed the goods. Companies need to think carefully about appearing on programmes which focus exclusively on the bad news.

In general, however, the media should be viewed as a potential friend rather than potential foe. It is important to establish and track its agenda. In the Shetlands, during the Braer disaster, we regularly mixed with reporters to find out what was concerning them and what news they expected to hear next. This helped to shape what was said at press conferences and written in press releases.

On another occasion we were helping a major pet food manufacturer which had received an extortion threat. The letter said unless £50,000 was paid into an account at the Halifax Building Society by a certain date, strychnine would be injected into a leading brand of dog food. A phial containing strychnine accompanied the letter to prove the extortionist had the poison.

This was different to the Tylenol situation because the crime had not yet been committed and, dare we say it, the threat was against dogs and not human beings. If the product were recalled as a precautionary measure the extortionist could have made the same threat to another of the company's products – where would it have ended? (This kind of extortion is often known as 'sweetmail' after a blackmailer in Japan, dubbed 'the man with 21 faces', repeatedly extracted large sums of money from a Japanese confectionery company, the size of Cadburys, until it eventually went bankrupt.)

If we told the media what was happening and the story was published, what would happen to sales of the product? Equally, if the news leaked out, the media would rip the company apart for putting profit above all else. We decided the media had to become an ally.

We agreed with officers from Scotland Yard to hold a joint press conference at which we would inform the media about the threat but ask them not to publish the story until the villain had been apprehended. Scotland Yard explained coverage of the threat would make it more difficult to apprehend the criminal, might encourage him to carry out the threat; and might encourage 'copycat' crime. In exchange, we would hold regular press briefings to keep reporters up-to-date with developments and they could, of course, publish the story once the extortionist had been caught.

There were no legal sanctions to prevent the media from publishing the story. There were no legal reasons to prevent them. But not one newspaper or broadcast medium used the story because, we believe, the reasons given to them were entirely plausible and reasonable.

In the event, the extortionist never carried out his threat to the pet food company but switched his target to Heinz Baby Foods. Dealing with a threat to babies is entirely different from dealing with a threat to dogs. The police mounted a huge surveillance campaign at every Halifax Building Society cash dispenser and eventually the criminal was apprehended. Only then did the story become national news.

Monitoring the media

As discussed in an earlier chapter, monitoring the media on a regular basis is one important way to spot evolving issues before they become full-blown crises – sometimes we call it 'crisis creep'.

But if it *has* hit the fan, monitoring what the media is saying about the situation is a crucial part of the response. If a serious factual error is broadcast or printed then no stone should be left unturned to have it corrected. Once a serious mistake appears in print or is stated on the broadcast media it becomes set in cement and repeated everywhere. In particular, it is important to remember the print media watch the broadcast media. Anything said on television or radio is likely to surface in newspaper stories. Financial journalists talk to fund managers and investment analysts. The lay media talk to the specialist media.

Retractions are difficult to obtain. The media doesn't like to admit it got it wrong. A published 'letter to the editor' does not carry anything like the same weight as the original article. The first thing to decide is whether the mistake is serious enough to make a fuss. If the error is only marginal a retraction or published letter to the editor may only serve to draw people's attention to the error again. If it is truly serious help should be sought from the Press Complaints Commission in the event of a newspaper error. If the error has been broadcast by one of the independent television companies it will be dealt with by the Independent Television Commission (ITC). If the ITC receives more than five complaints from the public about a programme or advertisement it has to investigate the complaint. If the BBC has perpetrated the error, the complaint should be lodged with its own internal watchdog. If none of these actions has the desired effect, threaten a lawsuit. If that doesn't work, go to court.

An eye for a *TV Eye*

In the early 1980s Rechem International, the specialist incinerator of toxic waste, ran into trouble when a farmer claimed his cows, which grazed close to the company's plant near Glasgow, had turned 'orange' and died. The farmer claimed the phenomenon was caused by toxins being emitted from the Rechem plant because toxic waste was being incinerated at the wrong temperature, for the wrong period of time. He also claimed £1 million in compensation.

Already the subject of local news reports, the situation became much more serious when two babies were born in the vicinity of the plant suffering from 'tiny eye syndrome' – a form of cancer. The mothers blamed the Rechem plant. The story became a national one.

TV Eye, the now defunct 'investigative' television documentary programme, decided to devote a whole edition to Rechem. The programme was notoriously biased against 'big business' so it was difficult to decide whether to participate in the programme or not.

In the end we advised the company to take part so it could present its side of the argument. We agreed to the company founder-managing director taking part in a pre-recorded interview.

We spent hours negotiating the parameters of the interview with the programme's producers. We made it clear our client would not talk about tiny eye syndrome since he was not a medical expert; in addition, we wanted assurance that negative views of the incineration process, to be given by an 'independent expert' from the US, were balanced by positive views from another independent expert whom we would identify.

Deeply suspicious of the programme's motives we alerted the ITC at an early stage about our worries. It was important to establish a relationship in the event we needed serious help later.

After many hours of rehearsal in television training studios, the day of the interview itself finally arrived. Just prior to the interview we re-established the parameters which we had agreed. We were told the interview would be filmed for some 30 minutes even though only some three minutes would eventually be used in the programme. This was not unusual but explains why, where possible, we prefer clients to be interviewed 'live'; provided they don't mess-up, ultimately you have more control over the final footage (see Chapter 11).

Within minutes of the interview beginning we noticed the interviewer reach for a sheaf of papers. Rechem's managing director was in the process of explaining how it was virtually impossible to incinerate toxic waste at the wrong temperature for the wrong period of time.

'How then', asked the interviewer as he handed the papers – on camera – to our client, 'do you explain this?' The papers were records stolen by a former employee of Rechem's Glasgow plant which seemed to indicate waste *had* been burnt at the wrong temperature for an incorrect period of time.

During rehearsal we had practised all the answers to the most difficult questions. Stolen records, however, had not been something any of us had anticipated. The managing director was completely thrown and went to pieces. Our dilemma then was whether or not to allow the interview to continue. Rightly or wrongly we decided to allow it to continue. We wanted to find out what other ammunition the programme had against the company; and were well aware of the potential horror of the PR man's voice saying 'that's enough' which would have been recorded and used in the programme.

Immediately after the recording we called Rechem's chairman to tell him what had happened. He dispatched us to Glasgow to investigate the stolen documents. They had, indeed, been stolen but on close examination of the case did not show evidence of incorrect incineration processing.

The programme was due to be broadcast in two days' time. Its producers would not hear of a second interview to 'set the record straight' so we contacted the ITC and explained our plight. ITC officials agreed to watch the programme in advance of broadcasting but would not allow us to be present at the viewing.

They conceded the balance of the programme was not fair but would not agree to the programme being postponed to allow a second interview to take place. Our only recourse was to furnish a written explanation which was spoken as well as seen during the programme. It was not entirely satisfactory but better than had originally seemed possible. If we had not taken this action, the programme would have said Rechem had refused to answer the charge.

An independent enquiry established that it was pure coincidence that the babies had been born with tiny eye syndrome. The farmer's cows had turned orange from eating ragwort. None the less, it had taken a frantic year of communications activity to help Rechem through its difficulty.

Summary

- The media cannot ever be ignored in crisis situations.
- Begin the communications process immediately.
- Crucial to the crisis response is for the CEO to be seen to take personal charge of the aftermath and to be the principal communicator – if he is good at it.
- In the aftermath, focus messages on how the organization feels about what has happened and what actions it is taking to remedy the situation.

- Establish the organization as the single authoritative source of information about what has happened and what is being done about it.
- Newspapers can be boycotted in the same way as other products.
- Think carefully before agreeing to appear on television programmes which focus on the bad news.
- Monitor the media constantly throughout the crisis; leave no stone unturned in obtaining retractions for seriously inaccurate reporting.

9

The legal perspective

When lawyers talk about the law normal human beings begin to think about something else.

former Private Eye editor Richard Ingrams

People are often quite rude about lawyers in crisis situations and, sometimes, this includes us. When we met with the chairman of Ultramar in the Shetlands one of his first questions was, 'Do we need to have a lawyer with us?' Our response was, 'Only on the end of the telephone'.

The problem can sometimes be that the training lawyers receive prepares them to think about crisis situations in a completely different way. Whereas we will advocate *telling it all, telling it fast and telling it truthfully*, lawyers will often advocate *saying nothing, doing nothing and admitting nothing*. What they don't always appreciate is the long-term consequences for an organization's reputation – and the knock-on effect on its financial bottom line. These can be far more damaging than any legal consequences.

Part of the trick is to get to the CEO of the company that is in trouble before the lawyer does. If he has already been in the hands of lawyers for several hours it often makes it more difficult to persuade him to take a more 'open' course of action. Sometimes it makes it impossible. The lawyers advising the company who owned the Bowbelle dredger, which tragically collided into the stern of the floating discotheque Marchioness on the Thames one summer's evening in 1989, drowning 51 young people, wouldn't even allow the Bowbelle's skipper to apologise publicly. The belief was saying 'sorry' amounted to an admission of liability.

This was blatant nonsense. Admitting sorrow does not mean the company is liable. What needs to be said is: 'We deeply regret this has happened and will leave no stone unturned in establishing the cause' – as Sir Michael Bishop did after the Kegworth airplane crash.

The intransigence of the lawyers, and the client's 'rabbit in the headlights' faith in all they said, caused us to walk away from the Bowbelle-Marchioness tragedy – one of the very few times we have done so in 20 years of advising companies in difficulty.

The other part of the trick is to marshall arguments in support of a particular course of action in the same way as lawyers do – by referring to precedents. Having a detailed knowledge of crisis case studies, of what worked well and what didn't, will provide evidence to support advice. In part, we hope this book helps in providing such evidence.

Legal pitfalls when communicating in crisis

From a legal standpoint there are two cardinal sins which must never be committed when communicating in a crisis. The first is *never to admit liability* for what has happened. There will always be an official investigation of some sort into what has happened and this will establish who is liable. The second is *never to speculate* about the cause of the crisis.

When something goes wrong, the first question from the media and others is: 'How on earth did this happen?' And this is the one question which will always be impossible to answer, not least because the answer will not be available. *What* has happened will be known but *how* it happened will not. As we have seen already, an essential part of the response is to describe what has happened.

Reporters will push hard for speculation about possible causes. Speculative theories make the story more interesting. They may try to flatter the spokesperson by suggesting he has been in the industry for a long time and, given the seniority of his position, must have some idea about the cause. The temptation is to think: 'Yes, I am a senior person with long experience and I won't look credible if I am clueless about possible causes'. This temptation must be resisted at all costs, for two reasons.

If the speculated cause proves to be incorrect it will be taken as a deliberate attempt by the organization to hide the true facts of the matter – in other words, it will be seen as a 'cover-up'. More importantly, there will be a clause somewhere in the organization's insurance policies which states the cause of any incident must be agreed with the insurers before it is made public. If it is not but is none the less made public, the insurance companies have the legal right not to meet subsequent claims.

In the aftermath of the Herald of Free Enterprise ferry tragedy, a senior spokesman for Townsend Thorensen, the ferry operator, fell famously into the speculation trap. And when we were advising the manufacturers of Cuprinol, the wood-staining and preservative product, during a crisis situation, we faced a huge dilemma with the company's insurers.

Herald of Free Enterprise

On 6 March 1987 The Herald of Free Enterprise, a cross-channel ferry operated by Townsend Thorensen, left Zeebrugge harbour in Belgium on a routine return voyage to Dover. Before the vessel had passed through the harbour exit it suddenly filled with water and turned over on to its side. The tragedy claimed the lives of 193 passengers and crew.

Shortly afterwards a senior executive from the company gave a television interview in which he was asked how the accident had happened. He speculated the ferry had 'hit the harbour wall' on its departure. 'Ferry hit the harbour wall' ran as the headline in newspapers for days. Thereafter the company battened down the hatches and gave few additional interviews, stating it had to deal with the operational aftermath of the tragedy.

This immediately made the media suspicious. The company's lack of communication prompted deeper investigation by reporters who soon established the ferry had not 'hit the harbour wall' but had sailed from Zeebrugge while closing its bow doors.

This caused huge quantities of water to enter the vessel and destabilize it. The media soon discovered Townsend Thorensen always operated their vessels in this way because it provided a quicker turn-round time at either end of the passage. Not only were accusations of a cover-up instantaneous but media reports claimed 193 people had died because of the company's 'corporate greed'. As with Pan Am after Lockerbie, the public lost confidence in the ferry operator and chose Sealink ferries instead.

The irony was that, just a few weeks before the tragedy, Townsend Thorensen had been acquired by the much bigger shipping line, P&O. The acquisition had been made largely because of the goodwill associated with the Townsend Thorensen name. After erosion of public confidence, however, P&O had no option but to paint out the name of Townsend Thorensen from vessel sides and replace it with its own. Townsend Thorensen, as an entity, vanished altogether.

Corporate manslaughter

As a case study, the Herald of Free Enterprise is important for another reason. It led to historic committal proceedings for manslaughter against P&O European Ferries (Dover) Ltd, four of the company's directors and three of its employees. This was only the second time in the UK that a charge of corporate manslaughter had been brought. It was first brought against a Welsh construction company in 1965 following the collapse of a bridge.

The charge of corporate manslaughter seeks to establish a link of 'recklessness' from the board director ultimately responsible for a particular activity through to 'coal face' operatives directly responsible for the failure. If proven it can lead to huge fines for the company and prison sentences for the individuals concerned.

The charges against P&O European Ferries alleged there was an obvious and serious risk that, as a result of the failure of the defendants to do their duties properly, the ferry would sail with its doors open, capsize and cause death. The prosecution alleged the defendants either gave no thought to the risk, or recognizing it, nevertheless went on to take it.

As in the case of the Welsh construction company the case was thrown out by the judge for lack of evidence. He said there was no direct evidence available to the prosecution that a reasonably prudent person in the defendants' position would have perceived the risk as obvious or serious.

The case had been widely seen as a test of whether or not a company could be prosecuted for manslaughter and the judge's decision had far-reaching implications for similar prosecutions in the future. Since then there has only been one successful prosecution – against the leisure activity centre which organised the fatal Lyme Bay canoe trip on March 22 1993 when four sixth-formers from Southway School, Plymouth, drowned.

Lyme Bay canoe tragedy

What started as a two-hour paddle to Charmouth, Dorset, ended in tragedy when the weather worsened and the canoes became swamped forcing the occupants into the water for hours. They had received only one hour's instruction in a swimming pool, had been in the canoes only once before, and the instructors had only the most basic of training. Most damaging of all, two former instructors had warned the leisure activity centre it lacked qualified canoe instructors and adequate equipment.

In December 1994 the managing director of the centre was jailed for three years and the company was fined £60,000. Eventually he was freed by the Court of Appeal after serving 14 months in prison.

The law was never intended to target small companies and there are now serious doubts as to whether it will ever be brought successfully against a large organization. In 1995, Thomson Holidays was informed that a similar charge against the company was being considered by the Crown Prosecution Service following the death of a holiday-maker from carbon monoxide poisoning. By February 1997 the company had still not been given a decision as to whether or not the case would proceed.

The Cuprinol case

Towards the end of the 1980s two men employed at Cuprinol's manufacturing plant in Frome, Somerset, died while at work. The deaths occurred within a few days of each other. Before they occurred other employees had complained of nausea and giddiness at the workplace.

The trade union representing the workforce claimed the deaths had been caused by inhalation of fumes from lindane, a chemical which had been used in the manufacture of Cuprinol but which had been banned by UK law for sometime. The trade union expressed its opinion to local radio and newspapers. *The Observer* ran a story and the issue became national news.

In situations like this, not unlike the Rechem International example, companies stand accused of a misdeed and are considered guilty until they are able to prove their innocence. We eyeballed the managing director and asked him if the accusations were true. He categorically denied the charge. The view from outside, however, would be: he would deny it, wouldn't he? No amount of protestation by the company will be believed by a sceptical outside world.

The only recourse in this kind of situation is to bring in respected, authoritative, outside experts, pay them to carry out an independent, objective investigation and agree to stand by their findings and recommendations. Third-party endorsement is usually the only strategy which works in such situations. But it can be lengthy and the recommendations may be expensive to implement.

As we discussed the third-party option with the company, its insurers said they agreed to an independent enquiry but would not agree to making public a promise to stand by the findings and recommendations. This was clearly because Cuprinol might claim against insurance policies for the cost of implementing any recommendations.

From a public relations standpoint it would have been suicide to announce an independent enquiry without promising to stand by the findings and to implement sensible recommendations. The ultimate decision rested with the managing director. To his credit, he went ahead with the announcement, promising, at a press conference, to implement any key findings.

The announcement bought the company a degree of time but it still had to deal with considerable press criticism as the enquiry findings were awaited. Three months later the experts reported no trace of lindane in the manufacturing process but found the factory to be inadequately ventilated. This had led to the sensations of nausea and dizziness experienced by the workforce. A coroner's court found the employees had died from unrelated causes.

The insurance company did not agree the factory was inadequately ventilated. It refused to fork out the £150,000 needed to make improvements. The company paid for the work itself – and changed insurers.

So what is the lawyer's role in a crisis?

It is about protection. Specifically, to protect:

- the company from criminal prosecution
- the company from future liability
- officers and employees
- the company's position with insurers and regulators
- documents.

In a crisis it is essential to preserve records of everything. There is a legal duty to preserve and eventually disclose in litigation relevant documents which are in the company's possession even if they are compromising or damaging. The legal process of 'discovery' demands all relevant documents to be handed over to officials investigating what has gone wrong, with the exception of 'legally privileged documents'. Legally privileged documents and communication are immune from discovery even, in some cases, from regulatory authorities.

There are two types of privilege, 'legal advice privilege' and 'litigation privilege'. Legal advice privilege is confidential communication between the client and his lawyer, whether the lawyer is from an independent firm or is the in-house counsel. Litigation privilege extends to confidential communication between the client or lawyer and third parties such as expert consultants, provided litigation has started or is in reasonable prospect.

Lawyers will advise companies to photograph or photocopy everything, particularly anything that may have to be removed by the company, the emergency services or regulators. It is also vital that any internal enquiry into an incident is led by a lawyer for it to have any legal standing. He will take detailed statements from employees, contractors and others involved in the incident as soon as possible and collect and secure any supporting documents or other form of evidence.

He may want to see press releases before they are issued. This is fine if the lawyer understands the public relations requirements of a crisis. We have, however, seen clear, constructive, communicative, not-legally-damaging press releases turned into meaningless gobbledegook at the hands of a lawyer. The writing of press releases is the preserve of the public relations professional. Advice may be needed from the lawyer on the approach but not on the words used. One final point: press releases may be produced in court after a crisis because they provide a useful – sometimes damaging – 'snapshot' of the company's position at the time of issue – so they *do* need to be accurate.

Compensation

Compensation for injured parties soon appears as an issue in newspaper stories covering a crisis. How much will be paid, by whom and how quickly?

A company that states publicly it will pay compensation to victims and their families is admitting liability for the event. So this must be avoided unless liability has been proven. On the other hand, any suggestion of callousness or complacency on the matter of compensation is out of the question. An appropriate response runs as follows:

> Of course compensation will be paid to people who have suffered – or their families if people have lost their lives – but how much and by whom will depend upon the outcome of the enquiry. We will do everything we can to ensure speedy payment of compensation by whoever is eventually found to be responsible for this tragic accident.

Ex-gratia payments

Affected families may face immediate financial hardship in the aftermath of an accident. It is wise for companies to have in place a policy – as well as a readily accessible budget – to make sums of money available to such families, for example to meet funeral expenses. These are called 'ex-gratia payments'.

Ex-gratia payments do not constitute admission of liability. They represent an act of helpfulness – and are seen as such. If, ultimately, the company that has made such payments is found not to be at fault it can reclaim its costs from the insurance companies of whoever is found to have been at fault. Never, however, reveal the amounts involved. They are a private matter between the company and families involved. This can be stated publicly in response to media questions on the subject.

Summary

- The long-term consequences for an organization's reputation, and subsequent knock-on impact on its bottom line, can be more damaging than any legal consequences.
- Expressing regret for what has happened does not constitute an admission of liability.
- Refer to precedents when arguing the communications case against the legal case.
- Never, ever admit liability unless it has been proven.
- Never, ever speculate about the cause.
- If accused, use authoritative third parties to demonstrate your innocence; your own protestations will rarely be sufficient.
- Don't dodge the compensation question.
- Be prepared to make ex-gratia payments; they don't constitute liability.
- Don't have blind faith in the advice of lawyers and insurance companies; they can get it wrong too.

10

Planning for the unexpected

Today my stockbroker tried to get me to buy some 10-year bonds. I told him: 'Young man, at this point I don't even buy green bananas'

US congressman when getting on in years

Executives, preoccupied with the market pressures of the present quarter, are not inclined to pay much attention to planning for future crises. However, it is instructive here to recall that Noah started building the ark *before* it began to rain.

Crises are often turning points in organizational life. They represent opportunities to establish a reputation for competence, to shape the organization and to tackle important issues. In most crises, because time is at a premium and resource allocation critical, company executives need strategic guidelines on what kinds of action are needed.

Calm and positive thinking

Taking action in a crisis can be fraught with risk. A strategy is needed for deciding when to define a situation as a crisis, when to take action and to work with others in solving the crisis. Such a strategic sense is in itself a great advantage when tension develops. The ability to keep cool when everything is collapsing is a quality valued in leaders, especially since apparent confidence by the leader is so reassuring to subordinates. Advance planning makes it more possible to concentrate on the actual problem when it peaks, and provides a framework for action.

Crisis management is about seizing the initiative – taking control of what has happened before it engulfs the organization. Planning to manage crises and issues is the key to corporate survival.

Those who are alert to the possibility that any event, even a crisis, is an opportunity to gain friends, to enlist support and, possibly, to attract new customers or shareholders, are well prepared to seize the initiative. Failure to have in place well-tried and tested contingency plans for every kind of emergency means, when the unexpected does occur, the company can only assume a combative posture; it is, of necessity, put into a defensive frame of mind.

Assuming a primarily defensive position establishes a negative attitude. It focuses thinking on reacting to conditions instead of the company acting on its own initiative. When a whole company is put into a negative frame of mind it is virtually certain to be seen as arrogant and unsympathetic to others – evidenced by Exxon Corporation's response to the Valdez oil spill. Instead, when positioned to deal not only with the crisis but also the inherent opportunities, a proactive posture can be established which leads to a positive attitude rather than a siege mentality.

Deeds versus declarations

A second principle, perhaps of even greater importance, is that deeds build a reputation far more effectively than words in advertisements or glossy brochures. In today's climate of corporate accountability, promises – words alone – are greeted with cynicism or disbelief. Such an approach actually creates a target for attack should the slightest lapse in performance occur. Nothing gladdens the public heart so much as a fall from grace by the excessively righteous. Self-aggrandisement campaigns lack credibility because everyone knows the sponsor accentuates the beauty spots and hides the warts.

A record of responsible deeds is a vital ingredient for a positive image. The essence of a good reputation rests not in trying to conjure up a good story to hide substandard performance, but in sensitizing management to the need to adjust performance so the deeds speak for themselves. The guiding principles of crisis management are to:

- develop a positive attitude towards crisis management
- bring performance throughout the organization into line with public expectation. Build credibility through a succession of responsible deeds
- seek and act on the opportunities during a crisis.

It boils down to deeds versus declarations. A record of responsible deeds is the organization's insurance policy when and if something goes wrong.

Planning to manage the crisis

Anything which can go wrong, will go wrong

Murphy's Law

The principles applying to crisis management planning are broadly the same for virtually all types of corporate crises. Methods for implementing the plan will not vary greatly for different types of crisis. It is usually impossible to anticipate every crisis which can arise but there are steps every company can take to prepare for one.

A coherent approach begins with the identification of potential crises. These may include:

- existing situations which have the potential to become crises
- crises which have beset the company in the past – or other companies in the same industry – and might recur
- planned activity which may meet with opposition from stakeholder groups.

The need is to catalogue the areas of risk: to assess the risk parameters. From this starting point it becomes easier to think through the logical series of steps which need to be taken in the crisis management planning process.

The audit process needs to be undertaken against our definition of a crisis in Chapter 6. The list then needs to be prioritized. A list which is too long will lose credibility with senior management. Since 'buy-in' from senior management is crucial to the whole process of crisis management planning, the list should be prioritized according to likely impact on the organization's financial bottom line. This will attract and sustain senior management attention.

Having identified likely areas of risk, the next questions to ask are:

1. Does the company have policies and procedures in place to prevent a risk from turning into a crisis?
2. Do plans exist for dealing with every aspect of the crisis should it occur?
3. Have the plans been tested to ensure they work satisfactorily?

Various supplementary, but equally important, questions may be added. For example:

4. Which are the audiences most likely to be affected by the identified potential crises?
5. Do plans include procedures for communicating effectively to these about what has happened and what is being done about it?
6. Have the communications aspects of the plan been tested, as well as the company's operational response?

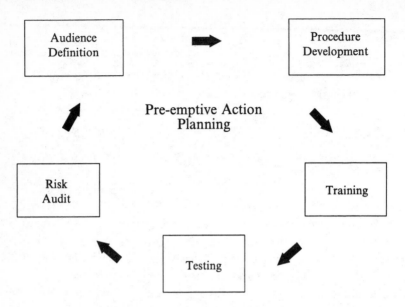

Figure 10.1 *Managing the process*

In short, planning for crisis management may be summarized as:

- *Cataloguing potential crisis situations.*
- *Devising policies for their prevention.*
- *Formulating strategies and tactics for dealing with each potential crisis.*
- *Identifying who will be affected by them.*
- *Devising effective communications channels to those affected so as to minimize damage to the organization's reputation.*
- *Testing everything.*

How to manage the process is shown in Figure 10.1.

Appointing the teams

To manage and contain the crisis, three separate teams will be required; the Core Committee, the Crisis Control Team and the Communication Team (the role of the Communication Team is discussed in the next chapter).

The Core Committee

This will comprise main board directors whose role is to take the 'high ground' of the crisis, considering such aspects as:

- business continuity; product sourcing and supply
- contingency budget approvals
- high-level communication with, for example, the overseas head office, government ministers and members of parliament
- content of messages for institutional investors, the media, customers, employees and other affected groups
- the insurance position; liaison with legal advisers; ex-gratia payments
- tracking what is happening to people; preparing to make hospital/family visits
- *above all*, ensuring the chairman or CEO is briefed and on his way to the site, accompanied by a public relations professional, as quickly as possible, to begin the media communication process.

Members of the team need to be grouped together in a 'war room' adequately equipped with telephones, fax machines, photocopiers, a television and radio (to monitor news reports) and boards around the room on which new information and decisions are recorded. The role of the log-keeper cannot be underestimated. He or she must be a long-standing company employee, intimately familiar with the business and its technical jargon but capable of writing clearly and succinctly in lay language.

It helps to have the boards inscribed with permanent headings so information can be clearly organized, for example:

People
Incident status
Environment
Weather
Product supply.

Each team member must be assigned specific, individual responsibility for these key functions. They must be aware of their responsibilities and to have rehearsed them. Each member of the Core Committee should have an 'alternate' in case someone is away. The team leader *must* chair regular information up-date meetings for all the team members, as often as every 15 minutes in a fast-moving situation.

The Crisis Control Team

The second team to come into play is the Crisis Control Team, responsible for the immediate 'hands on' operational response. The distinction between this team and the Core Committee is crucial. Neither should interfere with the other but the Crisis Control Team – which will be located at the site of the crisis – must keep the Core Committee constantly up-dated with developments. *It should have a member dedicated solely to this task*. Equally, the Core Committee – probably located at the head office – must provide the Crisis Control Team with strategic advice and rapid budget approvals for urgent areas of expenditure (see Figure 10.1, page 174).

The Crisis Control Team will also need a dedicated 'war room' for its members. Plans should include identification of an off-site 'war room' in case the site has had to be evacuated.

In addition to the materials and equipment already described, the 'war rooms' of each team should be equipped with plans depicting:

- locations of hazardous materials
- sources of safety equipment
- fire-water system and alternative source of water
- stocks of other types of fire extinguishers
- plant entrances and road systems, updated to include any road which is impassable
- assembly points and casualty centres
- location of plant in relation to the surrounding community
- areas affected or endangered
- deployment of emergency vehicles and personnel

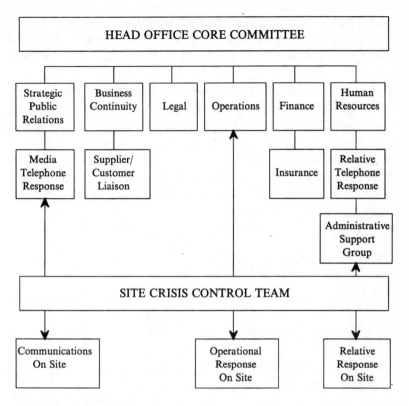

Source: Regester Larkin

Figure 10.2 *Responsibilities and interactions of crisis teams*

- areas where further problems may arise, eg, fractured pipelines
- area evacuated
- other relevant information.

Communication hardware

Since the unexpected tends to happen at Sunday lunchtime or on Christmas Eve, a comprehensive, fool-proof cascade call-out procedure is required with back-up alternates to stand in for key individuals who are not contactable. The cascade principle involves each member of the teams having the responsibility to call out at least two other team members once he or she has been called.

Facilities and hardware for communication need to be checked. Are key individuals equipped with mobile telephones or pagers? How would the switchboard cope with floods of additional telephone calls? (Occidental Oil took 4500 additional calls from the media and relatives in the first 24 hours after the Piper Alpha tragedy; Perrier took 3000, over the same period, in the UK alone – see Chapter 11 for advice on handling telephone calls.)

Crisis prevention

While it will be the responsibility of the Core Committee, Crisis Control and Communication Teams to manage and contain the crisis, yet another group of people is required to ensure the crisis doesn't happen in the first place – we call this the Crisis Prevention Team. Ideally, it should be made up from members of the other three teams. It doesn't come into play when the crisis occurs but should have been instrumental in minimizing the size of the crisis if it does occur – and in preparing and rehearsing the other teams to respond effectively when it does.

Crisis prevention team

This team formulates and sets company-wide policies appropriate to the hazards or risks of the business. It needs to ensure managers of each part of the business have the funds and other resources required to enable them to comply with policies – *as well as responsibility for implementing them.*

Such policies need to go beyond ensuring the organization merely complies with existing regulations. They must endeavour to anticipate 'worst case' scenarios. This approach is likely to prove more costly but the cost involved of not setting such far-reaching policies can prove catastrophic in terms of human lives and the company's entire future. Developing policies against agreed company criteria will help to give them shape and depth. Such criteria can be developed by answering the following questions:

- Would this situation really affect our bottom line?
- How realistic is the identified potential crisis situation?
- Could corporate action halt or moderate the crisis?
- Does the policy stand up to public scrutiny?
- Are the resources to act available?
- Is the *will* to act present?
- What would be the effect of inaction?

A positive approach to crisis management demands the implementation of preventative policies which have been developed and checked on a regular basis. Part of the Crisis Prevention Team's remit must be to conduct audits to check policy implementation.

Take, for example, a manufacturing company being audited for implementation of policies to prevent a physical crisis. Each year the audit group might select an audit programme which examines different topics – safety and loss prevention, air and water quality, solid waste disposal, occupational health and product quality.

Sites selected for audit can be based on their risk potential, their recent performance and the length of time since last audited. To lend weight to the audit process, the Crisis Prevention Team needs to report twice yearly to the main board on the status of the risk audit programme and measures required to minimize new areas of risk.

This audit process works well because it takes an objective view of each situation and ensures appropriate standards are applied across all divisions. The continuing interest displayed by the board gives authority to the Crisis Prevention Team and ensures divisional and local management corrects deficiencies.

Auditing for potential financial crises

The same audit process can be applied to potential financial risks. For example, the Crisis Prevention Team adopts the protagonist role of an unwanted bidder and looks for tell-tale signs of weakness in the company's performance which could make it an easy prey. The danger signals are likely to include:

- static or falling earnings
- poor return on capital
- unhealthy dividend policy
- bad cash management
- too high gearing
- poor investment policy
- too many, difficult to justify, rights issues
- unimaginative asset management (including well-stocked pension fund or cash mountain)
- neglected or poor communication with investors and their advisers
- major shareholder suddenly disposing of shares
- forthcoming tax or protectionist legislation
- business synergy with the predator (improved earnings prospects of the combined companies)
- marketing synergy
- knocking you out as direct competition
- acquiring your management team
- acquiring your production capacity.

External advisers – bankers, brokers and specialist public relations consultants – should be brought in to assist with the financial risk audit. Such advisers need to be reviewed regularly to ensure they are not also the advisers to potential predators.

The most important point to keep in mind is the worst case scenario approach. Organizations will rarely be criticized for considering every aspect of the situation and acting accordingly.

Appointment of the Crisis Prevention Team will demonstrate the organization's commitment to responsible management of its business. If it does its job effectively, the team will minimize the risk of a crisis occurring in the first place, will help to contain it if it should occur, will reduce the potential damage to the organization's reputation, and will change the organization's culture from responsive to positive. In summary, the role of the Crisis Prevention Team is to:

- Anticipate, clearly and comprehensively, all forms of crisis situations.
- Develop strategies and procedures for dealing with them.
- Check policies and procedures are implemented.
- Ensure they are rehearsed and updated on a regular basis.

Selecting team members

Various leadership styles emerge in crisis situations. While the 'human' participative manager is generally the most effective leader, he can sometimes inhibit the rapid decision taking required in an emergency. On the other hand, the authoritarian leader may act decisively at the expense of demotivating the team members and inhibiting creativity. It is vital for team leaders to recognize team members' different attributes and values and integrate them to maximum advantage during the crisis.

Members of all teams involved should be chosen for their personal qualities and talents – breadth of vision, ability to stay cool, knowledge of the company and its business, and the ability to make swift, clearly expressed decisions.

Some of the styles we have seen emerge include:

- *The 'ideas' person* – a creative member who is constantly injecting new ideas and suggestions. Some of these may be far-fetched but some may have real merit. It is vital for the leader to filter out the viable ideas and discard the remainder without discouraging the flow.
- *The communicator* – the individual who helps the flow of information both within and outside the team (not necessarily the team leader, although the team leader should possess strong communication skills also).
- *The doom merchant* – the devil's advocate who brings out the negative aspects of each proposed idea or solution.

- *The book-keeper* – the neat and orderly member who wants the records and logs maintained to perfection. This individual is more comfortable in such a role than as a decision maker. Nonetheless, it is a vital role.
- *The humanist* – the people-oriented member whose solutions always focus on the human aspects of the problem – an important visionary in the heat of the moment.

Putting the plan in writing

The importance of putting the plan in writing cannot be overestimated. In our experience, too often the communication plans do not exist at all – or exist in the heads of a few individuals. Companies must overcome the 'Joe will know what to do if it happens' syndrome; Joe may be on holiday – or dead. Even if he is available, he will be too busy to explain plans which should be readily available for all concerned.

Absence of a written plan will cause hours of additional work for an already fraught management. People will fail to take basic actions; for example, failure to notify employees in an emergency will lead to a flood of unnecessary phone calls about the effect of the incident on work schedules. Valuable time will be lost and tempers grow short because names and telephone numbers are not available when needed.

Checklists of things to do and people to contact are invaluable in enabling the organization to 'hit the ground running' when the crisis occurs. In a chaotic situation it's a huge relief to be able to hand to subordinates lists of things to do, giving assurance that all the essential steps will be taken.

The plan must not be too long or rigid. It must provide the flexibility and framework which acknowledges the unpredictable aspects of any crisis situation; and give management the leeway to use common sense. It needs a structure, but a loose one.

Put the plan in writing and assign a 'champion' to ensure it is kept up-to-date with changes to the business and movement of personnel.

Testing everything

Remaining familiar with the plan's content is always a problem. The best way is through crisis exercise simulations to test effectiveness of procedures and training. But first those with key roles should receive training. There is no situation more demoralizing than running an exercise in which everyone comprehensively screws up. Worse, it puts management off doing it again. No one likes to make a fool of themself.

A crucial ingredient to successful exercise simulations is getting the scenario right. Particularly if they have not previously participated in an exercise, management members will take part only reluctantly, believing they have 'more important things to do' and the whole business is a waste of time. If the scenario is in any way unrealistic they will refuse to continue and retire triumphant in the knowledge it *was* a waste of time.

When running the simulation, a good mechanism for making the mock incident evolve over real or imagined time is to feed in printed details of each new phase of the scenario and predetermined times.

For example, the person in charge of the response will receive a message stating:

> You have just learnt from the general manager of the company's manufacturing plant in Manchester that an explosion has taken place in or near the main chemicals storage depot. Several employees are unaccounted for, feared dead or injured in the wreckage. Reporters are arriving at the factory gate and many are phoning the company. The local MP is on the phone and wishes to speak to you urgently. Take appropriate action.

He will receive a series of such messages, sometimes at intervals of only a few minutes. He will then activate the Core Committee and Communication teams. Role-playing journalists, relatives, MPs, investors, investment analysts and environmental lobbyists start putting pressure on the company. Television camera crews arrive at the head office, as well as at the Manchester plant, demanding interviews. Every aspect of the company's response procedures is put to the test.

The simulation should last for four or five hours. It should conclude with a 'live', filmed press conference and be followed up with an immediate debrief on the response – a 'hot washup'. Later, a more considered written report should be produced clearly identifying agreed areas for improvement and whose responsibility it is for their implementation.

In our experience, those who have participated in the simulation generally rate their performance unrealistically highly. This is to be expected because of the sense of reality and unusual nature of the experience. A second evaluation needs to be provided, by qualified outside experts, which, while constructive, is more realistic. Simulations should be run once or twice a year to ensure recommendations from the previous one have been implemented and to take account of changes in the business and movement of personnel.

Summary

- Develop a positive attitude towards crisis management.
- Bring the organization's performance into line with public expectation.
- Build credibility through a succession of responsible deeds.
- Be prepared to act on the opportunities during a crisis.
- Appoint appropriate teams to prevent, manage and control crisis situations.
- Catalogue potential crisis situations.
- Devise policies for their prevention.
- Put the plan in writing.
- Test, test and test again.

11

Crisis communications management

The best-laid plans are worthless if they cannot be communicated.

Speed is of the essence. A crisis simply will not wait. Tell it all, tell it fast, tell it truthfully – and don't stop until the plague of locusts has had enough or found a richer source of food elsewhere. It's like wrestling a gorilla: you rest when the gorilla rests.

Stena Challenger grounding

What was so impressive about Stena Lines' handling of the media during the grounding of the Stena Challenger outside Calais in September 1995 was its speed of response to the media and the way in which the company organized the flow of information.

Although none of the passengers or crew was injured, media attention was acute because of previous ferry disasters. Unlike Townsend Thorensen, Stena did not clam up. Within two hours of the Stena Challenger hitting the sandbank the company was communicating with the media about how much food and drink was onboard: that plenty of telephone lines were available for the 172 passengers and 73 crew to contact anxious families; what it was doing to refloat the vessel.

In other words, the company concentrated on providing news about people first and, as we have seen, 'people' news must always take prominence over other information. It must be followed by news on the environment and property, if they have been affected, and lastly about money – what it is all going to cost.

The company's news handling deflected the media from focusing on questions about the navigation equipment and navigator; whether or not the skipper was drunk – as they did in the case of the Exxon Valdez. These are all questions it would have concentrated on in the absence of people-oriented news and, indeed, were asked later. But by this time the story had died and only marginal coverage was given to such issues. Stena had survived the crisis and, today, reports an increase in Stena Line passengers on the Dover-Calais route, with Stena Challenger carryings at normal levels.

A key to its successful response was its well-practised crisis management plan. A copy of the plan, with its practical information such as telephone numbers, contact points and clear procedures, is carried in the briefcases of the company's senior management in readiness for such an event.

The plan is activated by the master of any Stena Line ferry in distress: it is the master who puts into action an appeal for help. This produces a 'domino' effect at the company's headquarters in Ashford, Kent, with the ship and port management department which offers technical assistance necessary to manage the incident, and the four-strong public relations team who implement a media management plan. The public relations function ensures the ship management and technical teams are protected from media interference and can get on with rectifying the situation and ensuring passenger safety.

Background information to seize the initiative

The first 24 hours are critical. The 'information void' will be guaranteed to loom because of lack of hard facts about the incident. The void, however, can be bridged by offering the media background information on the company or installation which has been affected. This produces two results: the first is the creation of valuable breathing space to gather and check information about the incident before its release to the media; and it demonstrates to the media that the organization is clearly going to cooperate and communicate with it. Reporters who gather or telephone to cover the story will usually know nothing about the company, its plant and operations. Offering background information enables them to begin framing the story they will later write or broadcast.

So it is essential to keep updated background information packs about the organization and each installation or part of the operation considered potentially at risk. They should include:

- colour and black and white photographs
- diagrams
- basic information about
  - number of employees
  - how long in business
  - business description
  - names of key executives
  - safety record and practices.

Such packs located at the organization's headquarters as well as at each site at risk, where the media may descend in droves, will help the company to seize the initiative and prevent it from disappearing into the void.

Set up a press centre

It may not be possible, or advisable, to hold press conferences on company premises. Reconnaissance work needs to be done near each site considered at risk and arrangements made, perhaps with a local hotel, town or village hall, which could be quickly established as a centre for the media during the emergency. The media should be informed of the times of press conferences – and these must be adhered to. It will talk to other people between each conference but at least the company will have the opportunity to tell its own story once or twice a day, and to correct misinformation picked up by journalists. 1030 and 1530 are generally regarded as suitable times for holding press conferences because they meet the majority of deadlines.

Managing the press conference

This can be a nightmare. Hundreds of potentially hostile journalists gathered at one location have been enough to make grown men cry. Training and preparation are the keys. The press conference site should contain:

- external telephone lines and handsets
- a minimum of two fax machines
- two entrances, one for use by management and the other by the media
- a large diagram of the site or other visual aid material which will help to explain what has happened
- background information press packs
- refreshments (not alcohol)
- toilet facilities
- adequate security measures to ensure control of persons, either on or off site, with particular regard to their safety.

Useful tips to assist with the successful management of press conferences include:

- Restrict the numbers of the management team to only those with specific knowledge of different aspects of the incident; *never* fall into the 'comfort in numbers' trap at the top table since this only provides the media with more targets to snipe at. Ensure it is chaired by a senior company executive *provided* he or she is a good communicator.
- Place a time parameter on the conference if members of management need to get back to dealing with the problem in hand; *never* less than 30 minutes. End the conference at the specified time.
- Try and issue a new press release at the *conclusion* of the conference. Have copies placed strategically at the exit door for the media so they are encouraged to use it, allowing the management to exit via their own door.

Press conferences rarely work well on television. It is best to arrange one-to-one television interviews after the conference. Never exclude television cameras from the press conference however, as British Gas did famously when announcing the resignation of its much maligned chief executive, Cedric Brown, and the demerger of the company.

Although the company had arranged for one-to-one television interviews after the conference, broadcast journalists became infuriated when they and their cameras were excluded from the conference itself. Revenge was achieved by filming Cedric Brown leaving the conference, struggling to get through the throng of angry broadcast reporters, and being bonked on the head by a camera. A general picture of chaos – not helpful to the company's beleaguered reputation – was created which television companies delighted in showing the rest of the world on prime time news programmes.

Insist, however, that television cameras are situated at the back of the room and not allowed to gather round the table to get those nice close-up shots. This will only serve to further intimidate management and anger the print media who will not be able to see a thing.

There is another good reason for arranging television

interviews after the press conference. If someone has made a mess of answering questions during the press conference the television interview provides an opportunity to rectify the error. When we were in the Shetlands during the Braer disaster, the vessel's owner was asked at one press conference: 'In the light of what has happened will you in future route vessels through the narrow passage between the southern end of the islands and the north of Scotland?' He replied that thousands of vessels had plied this route for hundreds of years and saw no reason for changing it.

This was a big mistake. The next day, the *Today* newspaper covered its front page with a huge photograph of a pathetic-looking oiled seal beneath the caption: 'I'd do it again – Braer vessel owner'. However, before giving a television interview for the BBC after the press conference he was suitably admonished by his public relations adviser and proceeded to provide the correct answer during the television interview: 'We will look carefully at the findings and recommendations of the official enquiry into the accident and, of course, we will adopt any recommendations which improve safety and minimize damage to the environment'. Millions more people watch television than read newspapers so, to some extent, the mistake had been rectified.

A final point to remember about giving television interviews after the press conference is that the company may be besieged with requests for such interviews and may not be able to cope because of other pressures. If this is *genuinely* the case, and can be seen as such, the 'pooling' arrangement can come into play. 'Pooling' simply means explaining to the broadcast media that there is insufficient time to meet all its demands for interviews but the company is prepared to give one interview which the broadcast media can share. The media will select from among its numbers who is to conduct the interview and which film crew will be used. They then share the resulting footage or radio tape.

Dealing with the television interview

Training of television spokespeople is absolutely vital against crisis scenarios – partly to teach techniques and give confidence but also to discover who is good at it and who isn't. No company wants to saddle itself with a Lawrence Rawl.

Basic tips to remember are:

- prepare three main points which, if appropriate, refer to people first, damage to the environment or property second and financial consequences third
- if possible, rehearse the interview beforehand
- never speculate about the cause of the incident; instead say, 'The cause will be established once a full investigation has been completed'
- anticipate the worst possible questions and devise suitable answers
- praise the actions of third-party bodies, such as the police, fire brigade, etc
- never point the finger of blame at the company, employees or third parties
- eyeball the interviewer; never talk to the camera
- ensure the three main points are communicated irrespective of the questions asked
- jump on untruths, innuendo or misleading remarks immediately; interrupt if necessary.

Coping with hundreds of telephone calls

Few companies have more elaborate arrangements for dealing with incoming telephone calls from the media and relatives of employees than those in the oil industry. From our own experience of attempting and failing miserably to handle thousands of such telephone calls during one of the industry's worst disasters – at Bantry Bay in southwest Ireland, in January 1979, when an oil tanker, the Betelguese, blew up killing 50 people – we have helped the North Sea oil industry to pioneer a telephone response system which is today widely used by many of the utilities, airlines, chemical, pharmaceutical, engineering and food companies.

Since no company, whatever its industry, has a public relations or human resources department with sufficient people in it to cope with such pressure, the solution is to train employees from other disciplines within the organization in techniques for handling calls from these two vital audiences. Occidental Oil had a team of 40 trained responders in Aberdeen, and a back-up team of 20 in London, when the Piper Alpha production platform exploded late one evening in 1988. The teams helped the company to cope with some 4500 telephone calls during the first 24 hours.

Responding to media calls

Incoming telephone calls from the media will far outweigh the numbers of reporters able to get to the site. Sometimes there is nothing to see, only people to talk to, as in the case of a company collapse or fraudulent activity. Airplanes, ships and oil rigs can disappear altogether. So the telephone becomes an incredibly important channel of communication.

We advise companies to designate a media telephone response room equipped with sufficient handsets and its own dedicated telephone number which can be quickly issued via the wire services in the event of an emergency. This prevents the main switchboard from becoming jammed up and allows the normal business of the day to continue. It can be a meeting room in which the handsets are stored in a cupboard ready to be plugged into jackpoints around the room at a moment's notice.

Other items to be kept in readiness for the media telephone response teams include:

- pads of numbered log sheets for each team member
- a filing box for each individual
- flip charts and pens
- whiteboard and appropriate pens

- map of the affected site
- fax machine and photocopier
- refreshments
- 'Fast facts' file about the company and affected installation.

'Fast facts' is a term we coined to describe the media telephone team's equivalent to the background information pack. Written in conversational language and carefully indexed, it contains the answers to every anticipated question reporters might ask in a crisis situation. It also contains a list of questions about every conceivable kind of crisis the company may face so the answers can be filled in at the outset of the emergency. These questions act as an *aide-mémoire* to obtaining crucial information which may be forgotten in the heat of the moment.

A common mistake made by companies in crisis is to issue information to the media only via press releases. But, as we have seen, press releases can take a long time to prepare and distribute in crisis situations.

There must be a constant flow of information from the crisis management team's 'war room' to the media responders, so it is helpful to have the two teams located close to each other. Where this is not possible there needs to be an open telephone line between the 'war room' and the media responders so new information may be constantly accessed and passed on to media responders. New information, which is authorized for disclosure, is written on the whiteboards.

Whenever new information becomes available the supervisor in charge of the media response team – ideally a public relations professional although others can be trained in the role – gives the team a signal which means 'phones off the hook'. Responders finish their telephone conversations and the new information is gone through until every team member is confident about its meaning and comfortable with words to express the information.

Such briefing periods are also used to anticipate new questions which are bound to arise from the newly issued information. For example, the new information may state the site has been evacuated, but not where it has been evacuated to. The process of obtaining answers to these questions can begin immediately and, hopefully, be received before the question is even put.

Responding to calls from relatives

This is often the most ignored area of crisis communication management yet it is one of the most important, for two reasons. Any inability to respond sympathetically with information about employees to callers will only add to their anguish. And it will frustrate and anger the caller who may resort to calling a local or national newspaper thereby compounding the public relations problem.

It is also one of the most complex aspects of the crisis communications response. Few organizations have efficient systems for tracking who was on the site when it happened, although these are improving. But if the company is unable to confirm quickly whether or not an employee was present and provide the caller with information about his status, initial anger will turn to fury.

Many companies ask employees to fill in forms stating which family member should be notified in the event of something happening to the employee – but don't keep these records up-to-date. People's situations change and information may be given unwittingly to the wrong person.

When the Piper Alpha tragedy occurred Occidental Oil flew relatives of everyone who had been onboard the stricken platform to Aberdeen. It took over the Skean Dhu hotel at Aberdeen airport to accommodate everyone. Generous and correct though this action was, the company failed to keep track of who it was flying to Aberdeen. Some of the men working offshore were leading complicated lives and more than one wife claiming the same husband turned up the hotel. The rest is best left to the imagination.

When the questions come they are nearly always the same:

- Was he or she there when it happened?
- If he was is he all right?
- If he is uninjured where is he now and when can I expect to see/speak to him?
- If he has been injured, how serious are his injuries and which hospital has he been taken to?
- Will you help me to get there?

If the worst has happened and the employee has lost his life, this information must obviously never be given down the telephone. The police will want to inform the family but, if possible, they should be accompanied by a senior company representative.

British Airways EPIC Centre

The response system many companies employ to respond to relatives is modelled on British Airways' Emergency Public Information Centre (EPIC) near terminal four at Heathrow airport. It comprises a set of rooms only used when a plane has crashed or a crisis simulation test is being run. Because it is unique it is franchised out to other airlines.

Telephones are manned by flight attendants who have received additional training. A multiple language capability is important because of the different nationalities flying in aircraft. One bank of callers receive incoming calls, establish the name of the caller, who they are calling about, the nature of the relationship and where they can be reached. The caller is asked to wait by the phone until information can be given to them.

A second bank of responders establishes – in close coopera- tion with the British Transport Police located at Heathrow – the status of the passenger being enquired about and what information can be passed back to the relatives. Then follow all the logistical problems of flying relatives to hospitals and the scene of the accident.

In companies, the relative response team needs to be housed in a designated meeting room equipped in the same manner as the media responders. The two teams should not be located in the same room because of the different techniques employed. In essence, the media telephone response team is trying to give out as much accurate information as quickly as possible. The relative response team, initially at any rate, is trying to elicit information from callers.

Lack of resource may prevent using the double-banked system of British Airways, in which case one team will need to fulfil both functions. A separate administrative team should be set up, however, to deal with the logistics of getting family members to the hospital. The company will also need to ensure company representatives are at the hospital to assist family members.

The news release

The news release is a key communications tool in a crisis situation. It provides the company's official explanation of what is happening and may be used for expressing quotes from senior management on how it is 'feeling' about the situation. News releases should keep coming thick and fast throughout the crisis period.

A good idea is to number, time and date them, at the top of each release. This will enable journalists to keep tabs on the chronology of events more easily. It also enables media responders to ask which was the last news release seen by the journalist – and quickly ascertain the level of knowledge he currently possesses.

In some situations, it is worth thinking about who else the media will contact for information about the emergency, for example, the police, fire brigade, local hospital and other third party agencies. These can be sent copies of the company's releases in advance of sending them to the media. Such third parties are often less well geared up to respond to the media and will be grateful for copies of the company's releases to help with their own response. It helps also, of course, in attaining a consistency of message from all those involved. (In Scotland, the police have the right to vet all press releases concerning death and injury from an industrial accident.)

One final point. It is sometimes possible to prepare 'proforma holding statements' in anticipation of a potential crisis, for example in the case of a physical accident; here is an example.

PRESS STATEMENT

Date:

Time:

No:

XYZ Company confirms an incident (state what if known) has occurred (state where and when) and coordination of emergency rescue services is being controlled by the site's emergency committee.

Firm details about the incident are not yet known, but every possible action is being taken to safeguard lives and the environment.

Background information about the site is attached and more information about the incident will be released as soon as it becomes available.

The following special telephone number has been issued by XYZ Company for media enquiries relating to the incident...

-end-

Press statements should always announce news in the following order:

- nature of the incident
- location of the incident
- details of fatalities (numbers not names)
- details of injured (numbers not names)
- details of areas affected

- details of impact on the environment
- details of action to be taken for customers
- quote from senior manager expressing regret for incident and praise for those involved in all aspects of the emergency
- details about follow-up investigation into the cause of the incident
- reminder about site's safety record (if good) prior to the incident.

Keeping employees informed

Following a serious incident it is vital to keep employees informed of the situation and of developments. They should not learn new information via the media, as so often happens. Employees are the company's 'ambassadors' and need to be in a position to explain to customers, family and friends what is happening.

They should have access to company press statements prior to release. Where possible, briefings should be set up to provide an opportunity to ask questions; alternatively, they can be kept informed through e-mail, letters from senior management or printed newsletters. With employees it is important to obtain a sense of common ownership of the problem. Be honest and open about decisions being taken to solve the problem and share the entire remedial plan with them. Keep them updated regularly.

There should also be a policy in place which explains it is not the role of employees to talk to the media about the problem. It is impossible and would be wrong to try and 'gag' employees, but at least they will know what is expected of them if they are aware of the company's policy. This might run as follows:

> Should you be approached by a member of the press to comment about any aspect of the company's activities, please say you are not the best person to assist with their enquiry and the journalist should contact the press office.

The role of the emergency services

The police, in particular, can be of enormous assistance in crises of a physical nature. They can absorb some of the pressure through their own press and casualty bureaux working closely with the company involved in the emergency. They will also assume responsibility for ensuring bodies are identified by next of kin and for notifying families in the event of death caused by an industrial accident. Ideally, the police officer should be accompanied by a senior company representative so immediate condolences and assistance can be offered to the bereaved family. The police will not usually inform families of the injured unless the distances involved preclude the company from visiting the family. In most cases of injury, however, it is best to break the news by telephone so relatives can get to the hospital as quickly as possible.

The police will also be in attendance when survivors arrive at the hospital, or relatives and the media arrive at the site of the accident, to ensure control. They will organize traffic flows, establish meeting points, make secure the scene of the incident and organize appropriate resources.

It is important to remember that the police and representatives of the other emergency services involved in the situation, such as the fire brigade or HM Coastguard, will wish to communicate about what has happened; about the actions, bravery and equipment of their own men and women. The key is to ensure messages are coordinated and do not conflict with those being made by the company.

Company site managers should keep in regular contact with local police and fire brigades so relationships are maintained and roles defined. Informal agreements on lines of communication, wording of press releases and the release of new information can be drawn up. Sometimes it can be useful to invite a senior representative from the emergency services to attend company press conferences in order to present a 'united front'.

When it is all over

Experience is the name everyone gives to their mistakes

Oscar Wilde

In the aftermath of the crisis the temptation is to forget all about it as quickly as possible; to resume normal life. But surviving a crisis provides a huge opportunity for the organization to re-examine and reorganize itself to ensure it never again finds itself in a similar position. It can represent a turning point in organizational life, present opportunities to establish a reputation for caring and competence and rise from the ashes – chastened but in better shape to tackle the challenges of the age of corporate accountability. Never forget lightning *can* strike twice in the same place.

Attention needs to be given to employees and their families in the aftermath of crisis. Some may have been traumatized by the event. Some we know have left the organization because they could not face the possibility of a similar event happening again. Families who have been bereaved will often feel colossal anger towards the organization even though it may not have been at fault. The company can help by offering professional counselling. Sometimes it is possible to redirect anger felt for the loss of a loved one into a positive energy by channelling it into finding solutions to prevent the situation from ever occurring again; to make sense of what has happened by helping others in the future.

The continued inability of organizations – whatever their sphere of operations – to regulate their activities so the chance of crisis is minimized; a failure to check constantly that their deeds match their expectations and declarations; and lassitude over plans and preparations to deal with the worst, so that crisis can be quickly contained, must inevitably lead to greater constraints being placed upon organizations of all types.

The key to crisis management is crisis prevention, whether the vigilance and preparation is self-motivated or enforced by legislation. But if a fire does break out, comprehensive contingency planning can minimize the catastrophe; and a policy of open communication can minimize damage to corporate and individual reputations.

Summary

- Ensure all key players keep a copy of the crisis management plan with them at all times.
- Have background information prepared.
- Set up a press centre.
- Ensure executives are trained to manage successfully press conferences, television, radio and print media interviews – against crisis scenarios.
- Establish trained telephone response teams to cope with media and relative calls.
- Keep news releases coming thick and fast; date, time and number them.
- Don't forget employees – they are the company's 'ambassadors'.
- Coordinate the response of the company and third parties.
- When it's all over, review the organization from top to bottom in the light of lessons learnt – lightning *can* strike twice.

Bibliography

Ashley, W C and Morrison J L (1995) *Anticipatory Management*, Issue Action Publications Inc, Leesburg, Virginia, USA.

Brown, J K (1979) *This Business of Issues: Coping with Company's Environments*, Conference Board Report no 758.

Buchholz, R A (1988) 'Adjusting Corporations to the Realities of Public Interests and Policy', *Strategic Issues Management*.

Chase, W Howard (1984) *Issue Management: Origins of the Future*, Issue Action Publications Inc, Leesburg, Virginia, USA.

Chippendale, P and Horrie, C (1992) *Stick It Up Your Punter – the rise and fall of the Sun*, Mandarin Paperbacks, London.

Crable & Vibbert (1985) 'Managing Issues and Influencing Public Policy', *Public relations Review*, Summer 1985.

Forstner, G and Bales, J (1992/93) 'Building Dialogue into the Public Consultation Process', part 2, *Public Relations Quarterly*, winter.

Hainsworth, Brad E (1990) 'Issues Management: An Overview', *Public Relations Review*, vol 16 no 1.

Hainsworth, Brad E (1990) 'The Distribution of Advantages and Disadvantages', *Public Relations Review*, spring.

Hainsworth, Brad E and Meng, Max (1988) 'How Corporations Define Issues Management', *Public Relations Review*, winter.

Heath, R L and Nelson, R A (1986) *'Issues Management: Corporate Public Policy Making in an Information Society*, Sage, London.

Heath, R L and Cousino, K R (1990) 'Issues Management: End of First Decade Progress Report', *Public Relations Review*, vol 16 no 1.

Ito, Y (1993) *Beyond Agendas: New Directions in Communication Research from a Japanese Perspective*, Greenwood press, London.

Jones, Barrie L and Chase, W Howard (1979) 'Managing Public Policy Issues', *Public Relations Review*, summer.

Kinsdorf, Marion (1990) 'Crisis Management', *Public Relations Review*, vol 14 no 4.

Management Today, July 1994.

Meng, M B (1992) 'Early Identification Aids Issues Management', *Public Relations Journal*, March.

Meng, M B (1987) *Issues Management Today*, Unpublished thesis, Bingham Young University.

Mitroff, Ian and Pauchant, Thierry (1990) *We're So Big and Powerful, Nothing Bad Can Happen to Us, an investigation of America's crisis prone corporations*, Birch Lane Press, Secaucus, New Jersey.

Hanna, Nagy (1985) 'Strategic planning and Management: A Review of Recent Experiences', World Bank staff and working papers, no 751, Washington DC.

Post, J E and Kelley, P C (1988) 'Lessons from the Learning Curve: The Past, Present and Future of Issues Management', *Strategic Issues Management: How Organisations Influence and Respond to Public Interests and Policies*.

Sopow, Eli (1994) *The Critical Issues Audit*, Issue Action Publications Inc, Leesburg, Virginia, USA.

Taylor, Lord Justice (1990) 'The Hillsborough Stadium Disaster', Cm 962, 29 January.

Tucker, Kerry and Broom, Glen (1993) 'Managing Issues Acts as a Bridge to Strategic Planning', *Public Relations Journal*, November.

US Public Affairs Council (1978) *The Fundamentals of Issue Management*.

Wartick, S L and Rude, R E (1986) 'Issues Management: Corporate Fad or Corporate Function?', *California Management Review*, vol 24 no 1.

Welsh Economy Research Unit, University of Wales, Cardiff Business School and Welsh Institute of Rural Studies (1996) *The Economic Consequences of the Sea Empress Spillage*, July.

Index

References in italic indicate figures or tables.